WAKE UP AMERICA

ALSO BY KEISHA N. BLAIN

Until I Am Free:
Fannie Lou Hamer's Enduring Message to America

Four Hundred Souls:
A Community History of African America, 1619–2019 (coeditor)

To Turn the Whole World Over:
Black Women and Internationalism (coeditor)

Set the World on Fire:
Black Nationalist Women and the Global Struggle for Freedom

New Perspectives on the Black Intellectual Tradition (coeditor)

Charleston Syllabus:
Readings on Race, Racism, and Racial Violence (coeditor)

WAKE UP AMERICA

Black Women on the Future of Democracy

Edited by Keisha N. Blain

W. W. NORTON & COMPANY
Independent Publishers Since 1923

For information about permission to reproduce selections from this book,
write to Permissions, W. W. Norton & Company, Inc., 500 Fifth Avenue,
New York, NY 10110

For information about special discounts for bulk purchases, please contact
W. W. Norton Special Sales at specialsales@wwnorton.com or 800-233-4830

Manufacturing by Lake Book Manufacturing
Book design by Anna Oler

ISBN: 978-1-324-06560-9

W. W. Norton & Company, Inc.
500 Fifth Avenue, New York, N.Y. 10110
www.wwnorton.com

W. W. Norton & Company Ltd.
15 Carlisle Street, London W1D 3BS

1 2 3 4 5 6 7 8 9 0

*To the courageous Black women who fight
to save American democracy every day.*

CONTENTS

PART II: BUILDING POWER

WAKE UP AMERICA

INTRODUCTION

Keisha N. Blain

During the summer of 1968, the fifty-year-old civil rights activist Fannie Lou Hamer delivered a powerful speech on American democracy before a mostly white audience in Kentucky.[1] Hamer pointed to the undeniable fact that the United States had yet to live up to its promises. This was the crux of the problem at hand. In Hamer's vision, all Americans committed to social justice needed to address the unfinished work of building democracy. No American could look away as Black people fought for the recognition of their humanity. The struggle for civil rights was central to the fight for the future of American democracy because its health would depend on the fair treatment of all members of the American polity, not just some.

Hamer possessed a sense of urgency in conveying this message to white Americans about their role in building an inclusive and multiracial democracy. "We have a grave problem that's facing us today in this country and if we're going to make democracy a reality, we better start working now," she declared. White Americans could not simply sit on the sidelines or wait for progress to happen. They too needed to join the fight to save the nation. "It's time for us to wake up," Hamer advised members of the audience.[2]

Hamer's call for Americans to "wake up" is just as urgent today as it was during the 1960s. Despite the legal gains of the modern civil rights movement—namely, the 1964 Civil Rights Act, the 1965 Voting Rights Act, and the Civil Rights Act of 1968—the United States still fails to live up to the ideals of "life, liberty, and the pursuit of happiness." On the surface, there exists a veneer of equal voting access that might send the message that all Americans hold some political power. The phrase "of the people, by the people, for the people"—proclaimed by President Abraham Lincoln in his 1863 Gettysburg Address—still holds much currency in the American psyche. The problem, however, is that the day-to-day realities of Black and other marginalized peoples in the United States raise questions about the veracity of this mantra. A more detailed and honest examination of the United States—devoid of idealism and ideas of American exceptionalism—reveals a nation in need of urgent transformation.

Some of the social ills Hamer confronted during her lifetime remain with us today: voter suppression, economic inequality, and state-sanctioned violence, to name just a few that are covered in this collection. The attacks on our voting rights exacerbate the issues we face. In 2013 the Supreme Court's decision in *Shelby County v. Holder* greatly weakened the 1965 Voting Rights Act by undermining the use of preclearance—the process by which the federal government reviewed proposed changes to election law in states and counties that had a history of crafting legislation to block African Americans from the ballot box. Preclearance acted as a shield against the racist designs of state legislatures and politicians. Chief Justice John Roberts, in writing the majority opinion of the Court, reasoned that "our country has changed" since 1965, and therefore the jurisdictions covered by preclearance no longer merited the extra scrutiny.[3] Since then multiple state and local authorities have demonstrated the fallacy of Roberts's ruling. They immediately chipped away at the Voting Rights Act, thereby undermining the protections that would ensure full voting access for marginalized U.S. citizens.[4]

This winnowing of equal representation is further compounded by the startling racial wealth gap in the United States. Two hundred and fifty years of enslavement followed by another 150 years of racist and exclusionary practices, including Jim Crow and redlining, deepened economic inequality in Black communities across the nation. As a group of researchers at the Brookings Institution recently concluded, "Wealth was taken from [Black] communities before it had the opportunity to grow."[5] And little has been done to improve these disparities, as demonstrated in a 2018 report by University of Bonn economists Moritz Kuhn, Moritz Schularick, and Ulrike I. Steins. They concluded that "no progress has been made in reducing income and wealth inequalities between black and white households over the past 70 years."[6] It is therefore not surprising that a typical white family in the United States today has a median net worth of $171,000, nearly ten times greater than that of a typical Black family.[7] This stark racial disparity has fundamentally shaped the experiences of Black people as the barriers to accumulating wealth have impeded opportunities in every sector of society.

In addition to wealth inequalities and unequal voting access, Black Americans must contend with unjust police killings. The systemic problem of police violence and brutality in Black communities across the nation mirrors the pervasive acts of lynchings during the Jim Crow era. Over the past few years alone, we have witnessed unrelenting acts of violence against Black people—at the hands of white supremacists and even by those who have sworn to "protect and serve." As a 2019 report revealed, police violence is now one of the leading causes of death for Black American men.[8] Black women and girls are also vulnerable to police violence, as the African American Political Forum's 2015 "Say Her Name" report makes clear.[9]

The challenges facing Black communities today—built upon centuries of discrimination—extend to health and education. As disparities in maternal mortality rates and the disproportionate impact of COVID-19 diagnoses and deaths reveal, Black Americans experience poorer health care access and lower quality of care than white Americans.[10] In the realm of education, school districts with mostly white students receive significantly greater resources than do districts with mostly students of color.[11] In recent years, the teaching of African American history has come under attack, as evidenced by the Florida Department of Education's declaration that the AP course on African American studies "lacks educational value."[12] Its decision arrived after conservatives led a nationwide campaign to supposedly rid elementary and secondary classrooms of "critical race theory," even though it was not being taught there, and of "divisive concepts" in general.[13]

Conservative politicians have also put in place bills to curtail information to students and the public. While they have crafted numerous arguments to justify their actions, this censorship is an affront to democracy. Florida's Stop WOKE Act, its "Don't Say Gay" law, and similar discriminatory efforts violate the First Amendment of the Constitution and therefore undermine the very essence of democracy. The essays in this book grapple with these concerns as well as with other challenges that threaten the future of American democracy, including anti-LBGTQ+ violence, misogynoir, ableism, fatphobia, and anti-Blackness.

We need to find a promising way forward. How might we work together to build an inclusive and multiracial democracy that lives up to the ideals and promises of the nation's founding documents? What concrete steps can we take—as ordinary citizens, policy makers, activists, influencers, and leaders—to make our democracy stronger? This collection brings together some of the nation's foremost progressive Black women politicians, activists, and intellectuals to answer these questions. The writers offer concrete proposals for strengthening American democracy, organized around three core themes: claiming rights, building power, and combating hate.

On the importance of Black people and other marginalized people claiming civil and human rights, we hear from Carol Moseley Braun, the first African American woman elected to serve in the U.S. Senate; Laphonza Butler, a senator from California and president of EMILYs List; Taifa Smith Butler, president of Demos; Rep. Sheila Jackson Lee (D-TX); disability consultant and impact producer Andraéa LaVant; Atima Omara, former president of the Young Democrats of America; disability rights advocate Vilissa Thompson; and transgender rights activist Raquel Willis.

Part II shifts focus to the theme of building political and economic power. It underscores the significance of individual and collective power in sustaining a healthy democracy. In this part, we hear from Aimee Allison, president of She the People; public health advocate Dr. Rhea Boyd; veteran political strategist Donna Brazile; Glynda C. Carr, president and CEO of Higher Heights of America; Black Lives Matter co-founder Alicia Garza; New York City Council member Crystal Hudson; Kim Michelle Janey, former mayor of Boston; abolitionist Mariame Kaba; and former Ohio state senator Nina Turner.

Part III grapples with the theme of hate, an ever-growing threat to American democracy. Here the writers Charlene A. Carruthers, founding national director of BYP100 (Black Youth Project 100); Renée Graham, columnist for *The Boston Globe*; Rev. Dr. Jacqui Lewis, senior minister at the Middle Church; Rep. Ruth Richardson (D-MN); and Tami Sawyer, former Shelby County commissioner, underscore the necessity of eliminating all forms of hate in American society as a vital step in building a strong democracy.

This timely, multigenerational book offers a snapshot of the ideas of some of the nation's most influential thinkers and change makers. It captures the dynamism of Black women's political leadership and centers voices that have historically been silenced, including those of younger activists, radical organizers, and people from the queer and disabled communities. Drawing from their diverse experiences and expertise, the Black women in this collection offer critical insights on how we can effectively build a more inclusive and equitable society.

With the 2024 U.S. presidential election on the horizon, I invited these women to contribute to this collection because of their records of impactful work at the grassroots, national, and international levels. These writers, representing diverse socioeconomic backgrounds and religious beliefs, capture the depth and richness of Black women's wisdom and radical visions for transforming American society. In the spirit of Fannie Lou Hamer, the Black women leaders featured in these pages call on Americans to "wake up"—to acknowledge that we have considerable work to do to build a democracy that embraces all Americans, regardless of their race, gender, sexuality, ability, socioeconomic background, or any other social category. They embody another aspect of Hamer's enduring legacy as well by following the example she set as a bold and courageous truth-teller who never minced words about the urgent need for change. Taking up Hamer's mantle, they hold fast to the belief that change is possible and offer concrete recommendations on how to make these visions a reality. Their words of wisdom are especially timely at this moment in our nation's history.

Because they occupy a marginalized position—shouldering multiple and intersecting forms of oppression, including racism, sexism, and classism—Black women are uniquely positioned to combat injustices in our society. Not surprisingly, they have used whatever was at their disposal to influence politics and guide U.S.—and even global—policy. As the most subordinate group within racial and gender hierarchies, Black women have understood, perhaps more than others, what it means to live without full citizenship and human rights. By articulating a vision of freedom for themselves, Black women are also advocating for the liberation of all oppressed people.[14] Their political advocacy—and their efforts to strengthen American democracy—therefore broadens the rights and opportunities for every person in the United States.

Today Black women represent one of the most consistent—and therefore powerful—voting blocs in the nation. In 2008 and 2012, Black women voted at the highest rate of any race and gender subgroup. Their votes—96 percent of them cast for President Barack Obama—played a vital part in his reelection in 2012.[15] Black women voters backed the then-incumbent in several key battleground states—Ohio, Pennsylvania, and Florida—that together gave Obama sixty-seven Electoral College votes.[16] While Black voters in general had high turnouts in prior elections, Black women often led at higher rates than Black men and other racial and ethnic groups in the country.[17] And their absence was felt in 2016 when the Black voter turnout rate declined for the first time in twenty years.[18] Though fewer Black voters made it to the polls that year, Black women still left their mark, as an estimated 63.7 percent voted—one of the year's largest voter turnout rates compared to other racial groups.[19] And they were instrumental in helping the Democratic presidential candidate Hillary Clinton win the popular vote: 94 percent of Black women voted for the former U.S. secretary of state and former first lady.[20]

Black women's robust participation in electoral and grassroots politics today stems from a long history of exclusion and marginalization that they have been passionately resisting for centuries. In eighteenth-century Massachusetts, for example, Elizabeth Freeman, an enslaved Black woman, sued for her freedom on the basis that the state constitution guaranteed of equal rights for all. She won her case in 1781.[21] In the aftermath of the Revolutionary War, free Black women across the country devised a range of strategies to challenge their exclusion from various aspects of society. Many turned to Black churches as crucial spaces where they could organize and demand the expansion of their political and citizenship rights.

By the early twentieth century, a cadre of Black women leaders rose to national prominence as they sought inclusion in the struggle for woman suffrage. Ida B. Wells-Barnett—one of the most significant early civil rights activists—called for federal legislation to stop the lynching of Black people, a critical domestic challenge. Her commitment to ending racist violence in the United States laid the groundwork for the passage of federal anti-lynching legislation—a process that would take more than a century to complete.[22] From the 1920s to the '50s, Black radical women—including Black nationalists and women on the Communist Left—worked to expand the fight for citizenship rights beyond issues of racial violence and white supremacy to include demands for better health care, housing, education, and more.[23]

In the 1960s and '70s, civil rights and Black Power activists built upon the legacies of earlier generations to lead a national movement to increase civil and human rights for Black Americans. Black women—including Hamer, Septima Clark, Ella Baker, Gloria Richardson, and Angela Davis—were at the forefront of these efforts. These women recognized the flaws in American democracy, but they believed the United States was worth saving. They often looked to the nation's founding documents—the Declaration of Independence and the U.S. Constitution, including the Bill of Rights—to reaffirm their demands for equal participation and equal access. Since then, numerous Black women leaders and activists—Stacey Abrams, Ayanna Pressley, LaTosha Brown, Imara Jones, Bree Newsome, Ayọ (formerly Opal) Tometi, Andrea Jenkins, Cori Bush, and many more—have been unwavering in their advocacy for the expanded rights and freedom of marginalized groups.

Black women activists, intellectuals, and leaders have been creating strategies and amplifying them at the local, national, and transnational levels. *Wake Up America: Black Women on the Future of Democracy* brings together twenty-two of today's leading progressive Black women to offer key reflections on some of our nation's most pressing challenges. Here they give their singular and valuable perspectives and offer vibrant ideas and solutions to benefit democracy on our shores and around the world. They don't all agree on the necessary steps to make an inclusive democracy a reality. Some support reform—making changes to existing structures—while others advocate abolition, the complete dismantling of these structures. Some call for more opportunities for Black women in politics—arguing that gaining greater representation and a "seat at the table" will open more doors of opportunity for them to shape public policy. Others propose more revolutionary responses, including a desire to overturn the proverbial table and create alternative spaces of power. Some writers look primarily to the law and public policy as the bedrocks on which to build a stronger democracy. Others emphasize the need to focus on changing culture—including media and entertainment—as the crucial avenue for shifting the hearts and minds of all Americans.

While they all offer distinct proposals, the Black women in this collection agree that it's time for Americans to "wake up" and commit themselves to dismantling systems of oppression that undermine the future of democracy. And they all argue that change is possible—as long as we are unwavering in the fight. My hope is that for those of you who are committed to making democracy a reality in the United States, their incisive commentary will provide a blueprint for steps we can take right now and in the years to come.

Part I

CLAIMING RIGHTS

ON WOMEN'S RIGHTS

Hon. Carol Moseley Braun

Intersectionality, a term introduced by legal scholar Kimberlé Crenshaw in 1989, captures the interconnections of race, gender, class, and other social categories.[1] As a concept, it is more straightforward than any lived reality. When you are Black, female, and working class, these identities come together in unpredictable ways.

Throughout my career, I have attempted to chart the different stereotypes and popular conceptions pertaining to all three, and I have run into a miasma of complementary—but sometimes contradictory—expectations. These booby traps and stereotypes were hard to ignore. They were all designed to remove or limit my agency—on the basis of my gender, race, or class status. They are a reality that all Black women in the United States face.

The stereotypes stem from the same societal—and sometimes legal—concepts that justified slavery and the treatment of women as infantile beings. The common law idea of coverture, which can be traced back to the Middle Ages, held that certain people did not have the intellectual capacity to make decisions for themselves, much less for the broader society. On the basis of coverture, women were denied the opportunity to own property, to stand in civil society in their own right, to file lawsuits, or to even have a voice in public affairs. This was an inherent part of the foundations of the United States despite the soaring words of the 1776 Declaration of Independence: "We hold these truths to be self-evident, that all men are created equal, that they are endowed by their creator with certain unalienable rights, that among these are life, liberty, and the pursuit of happiness."

Our current challenge in the United States is that these words have not yet been fully realized. We must press ahead and push the envelope in every possible way to expand opportunities for all Americans, especially those who are marginalized. This is the only way we can make the words of the Declaration of Independence finally true.

The history of the United States has been the constant struggle, sometimes in fits and starts, toward making the words of the Declaration of Independence reflect the reality of American society—and not simply myths about her people. We live in a nation where stereotypes and assumptions continue to dominate public discourse. Women are not to be trusted. Black people are shady, if not criminal. Indigenous people no longer exist. Poor people are to be punished for some spiritual transgression. All these false statements and more have become justifications for oppression and exploitation.

The American nation was built on the labors of enslaved people, the subjugation of women, and the displacement of Indigenous people who had been here long before Europeans arrived.

Yet the founders justified their obvious hypocrisy on the basis of tradition and the law. For so many, equality was never "self-evident," and the denial of their agency is one of the most troubling aspects of the foundation of this great nation.

Some early Americans saw the contradictions and even pointed them out, notably Abigail Adams, the wife of John Adams, one of the nation's Founding Fathers. In her famous letter to her husband, dated March 31, 1776, Abigail Adams implored, "I desire you would Remember the ladies, and be more generous and favourable to them than your ancestors. Do not put such unlimited power into the hands of the Husbands."[2] In an earlier letter, dated September 22, 1774, she affirmed her commitment to abolition: "I wish most sincerely there was not a Slave in the province. It allways appeard a most iniquitious Scheme to me. Fight ourselfs [*sic*] for what we are daily robbing and plundering from those who have as good a right to freedom as we have."[3]

During the 1770s, at a time when most of her contemporaries upheld racist and sexist views, Abigail Adams interceded on behalf of women and the enslaved—in ways that distinguish her even today. From a modern perspective, she was a feminist, a champion of women's rights and equality under the law, and a critical thinker. She did not shy away from pointing out her husband's hypocrisy—she noted the gap between his words and his deeds.[4]

Much has changed since the 1770s, but too many things remain the same. Black women today shoulder what sociologist Moya Bailey refers to as *misogynoir*, a term that speaks to the overlap between racist and sexist stereotypes. A combination of the term *misogyny* and the French word for Black (*noir*), misogynoir addresses the special brand of oppression and discrimination that Black women face on a daily basis.[5] Black women navigate multiple stereotypes at once: we are often undervalued as women and discounted as Black Americans. Others question our abilities and our motives. Where a white man starts out with a presumption of competence as part of his privilege, a Black woman must dismantle each stereotype brick by brick before she can be taken seriously. It is the difference between natural authority and earned authority.

These stereotypes come together to shape human interactions, and they diminish the opportunities—or lack thereof—that Black Americans and women receive. I know this from personal experience. In 1992 I was elected to the U.S. Senate. Of the 1,806 senators who had been elected since 1789, I was the first Black woman. I was the first woman to be appointed to serve on the powerful Senate Finance Committee, an appointment that was such an outlier that many presumed it was an accident.

I have agitated for civil rights and equality for my entire adulthood—I even marched with Rev. Dr. Martin Luther King, Jr. However, it was not until the 1970s, when I became an assistant U.S. attorney, that I encountered misogynoir firsthand. While working late one evening on a trial, I went to catch a taxi in front of the Federal Building in Chicago. After a few minutes, a police car pulled up in front of me, and the policeman on the passenger side of the car leaned out and yelled, "Hey, you! Give up that corner!" I had no idea what he was referring to. The police car then pulled away. I continued to wait for a cab, even though several had already passed by me. Meanwhile the police car drove around the block and pulled up to the curb again. "I told you to give up that corner!" the same officer yelled out. Only then did I figure out that the officers assumed I was a prostitute looking for work. Fuming, I considered that if I allowed myself to get arrested, I could start a scene, equipped as I was with my U.S. attorney badge in my purse. But just then a taxi finally stopped for me, and I had to make a split-second decision: get arrested or go home. I chose to go home.

Black women in the United States are routinely treated with disrespect and assumed to be lesser than others in ways that can be life threatening. That night in Chicago I dodged a bullet because it was far more important to me to continue the trial than to confront a policeman.

The good news is that change is constant. Attitudes and circumstances change, so it is unlikely that I would have the same experience today that I had during the early 1970s. Changes in attitudes set different expectations.

Neither my mother nor my grandmother could have conceived of a debate about whether a Black man or a white woman should be the next president of the United States. Yet this was the reality we faced as a nation in 2008. We can now look back and reflect on the election of Barack Obama, the first Black president. He, in turn, appointed his former opponent to the position of secretary of state. In our nation, same-sex and interracial marriages are legal—evidence of some of the changes that have taken place over the last few decades. This progress speaks well about who we are as a society. We can become better if we are determined to do so.

The march of history still moves forward, even though it is not linear, and there is still much we can do to improve this nation. For starters, we must ensure that women, Black people, poor people, and other marginalized groups have the same rights and opportunities that white men enjoy. Women are entitled, as a function of their humanity, to enjoy the same rights and opportunities as men; Black people and other people of color, for the same reason, are entitled to enjoy the same rights and opportunities as white Americans. This is necessary if we hope to build an inclusive democracy. In the "land of opportunity," we should make every effort to extend help and support to those who have been relegated to the bottom of the socioeconomic ladder. All Americans should have equal access to the resources they need not simply to survive but to thrive in this country.

If we refuse to allow stereotypes to shape our judgment of people, we will unleash opportunity for real change. The poor cannot change their circumstances alone—it requires a community effort and a recognition that poverty hamstrings us all. Women, Black people, and other marginalized Americans will move beyond being the first in any field when we take off the shackles restricting opportunity and embrace the contributions and talents of every single individual. This is the change we desperately need in the United States to create a better future for us all.

My young niece once declared, "But Auntie Carol, all the presidents are boys." I believe her generation will change this reality. And the centuries of women's efforts to break free of the bonds of coverture will finally pay off. We can—and will—build a nation that truly reflects the ideals of the Declaration of Independence: "life, liberty, and the pursuit of happiness."

ON REPRODUCTIVE FREEDOM

Hon. Laphonza Butler

It is telling that Fannie Lou Hamer, Mississippi's greatest voting rights icon, was the victim of a nonconsensual hysterectomy. In the rural South in the 1960s, the practice was so commonly performed on poor Black women that it was nicknamed a "Mississippi appendectomy."[1] Its ubiquity was a sign of just how little control Black women had over their own bodies.

Mississippi has long played a peculiar role in our nation's history. I know it well. I grew up in Magnolia, Mississippi, the granddaughter of Louisiana sharecroppers. My mom raised three kids while caring for an ailing husband who died too soon. I studied at Jackson State University, where I learned about Hamer and other civil rights leaders as well as Mississippi's history of enslavement and emancipation, Reconstruction, Jim Crow, and the fight for voting rights. After leaving Mississippi, I worked with low-wage working women, nursing home and home care workers, and security guards who were organizing unions for the first time to demand dignity and respect on the job. I have seen and been a part of many victories, from raising the minimum wage and securing critical agreements on behalf of these workers to helping women win office. I know firsthand that progress is difficult to achieve, but it does happen. And I know that the pendulum of freedom swings vigorously.

So I wasn't the least bit surprised when the U.S. Supreme Court decided to take up *Dobbs v. Jackson Women's Health Organization*—a case that originated in Mississippi, where maternal mortality rates, especially for Black women, are among the highest in the country. For all that changes, some things remain the same.

Dobbs centered on a 2018 law that banned most abortions in Mississippi and targeted the state's only licensed abortion clinic. By 2022, the conservative majority on the Supreme Court had grown to a 6–3 advantage, and it was clear that the fifty-year precedent protecting women's reproductive rights was in jeopardy. The history of Mississippi offers multiple examples of attempts to deny rights to its residents—a tradition the state proudly carries on today.

It's tempting to just give up on Mississippi. After all, the state seems to reflect and amplify the worst impulses of the American tradition. It leads the nation in nearly every negative category. According to the Centers for Disease Control and Prevention (CDC), Mississippi "had an infant mortality rate of 8.12 per 1,000 live births, well above the national average of 5.42 in 2020, the most recent year for which the national data is available."[2] Moreover, "Black babies are twice as likely to die as their white counterparts in Mississippi." The state's "rate of maternal mortality of 22.1 per 100,000 live births is well above the national average of 17.4," and "Black women in the state are affected more than other racial groups (51.9 deaths per 100,000 compared to 18 for white women)."[3]

What happens in Mississippi has an uncanny ability to reverberate elsewhere. This was very much on my mind in 2022 when the draft of the *Dobbs* opinion leaked. The historical experience of Black women has forged in us a perspective grounded in the undeniable connection between equal participation in democracy and control over one's physical self. This truth has provided a fortitude that has withstood the worst of our country's history, and it also provides a roadmap for confronting our challenges today.

While a few more months would pass before the Court issued its final decision, the draft opinion revealed its hand. It gutted *Roe v. Wade* by allowing state governments to decide whether abortion is legal.

Once the Court issued its decision, some states went on to reaffirm the right to an abortion. However, twenty-six states had already decided, long before the Court decision, to ban abortions in most or all circumstances.[4] A majority of those states are in the South, still home to the country's largest concentration of Black people. This means that more Black women live in states that are likely to ban abortion than in states that recognize its legality. Such is certainly the case in Mississippi where, according to recent census data, Black people make up about 38 percent of the population, compared to about 13 percent of the U.S. population overall. Across the country nearly 6 million Black women will be harmed by these abortion bans.[5]

Banning abortion will widen the already stark differences in health care outcomes for Black women. The CDC has found that Black and Indigenous people are two to four times more likely than white people to die during pregnancy or around the time of childbirth.[6] Moreover, women who are forced to have an unwanted pregnancy are more likely to be in poverty and experience financial distress for years afterward.[7] Along with economic disparities, Black women face inequalities in access to health insurance, contraceptive care, sexual and reproductive health care, and maternity care, and in health care outcomes.[8]

Even when our rights are not under attack, policy makers have limited our abortion access by making it logistically impossible. Elected officials at all levels have tried to implement increasingly creative ways to limit or end access to abortion, from trying to drive providers out of certain states to making the process onerous to even citing flawed science. This is why our fight is about more than just winning our rights back; it is about upholding reproductive justice through equitable access.

At the time of the *Dobbs* leak, I had recently become president of EMILYs List, the nation's largest resource for women in politics that has helped elect more than seventeen hundred Democratic pro-choice women throughout its history. I was its first Black president and its first mom. Now the very rights EMILYs List was founded to protect faced certain judicial doom, and I had to confront that fact.

The leaked opinion was published the day before the organization's largest annual event in Washington, D.C., called We Are EMILY. The hours leading up to it were tense. Women everywhere were outraged—an outpouring of righteous anger could be seen and heard across the country. At our event, Vice President Kamala Harris channeled all the rage in the room as she declared, "Some Republican leaders are trying to weaponize the use of the law against women. How dare they? How dare they tell a woman what she can and cannot do with her own body? How dare they try to stop her from determining her own future? How dare they try to deny women their rights and their freedoms?"[9] Yes, how dare they? I felt the same outrage.

The attack on women's rights and the overturning of *Roe v. Wade* didn't happen in a vacuum. Republicans had been trying to roll back our rights and our access to abortion for decades. In the

wake of Donald Trump's presidency, they were rolling back voting rights, denying election outcomes, threatening gay and trans
rights, and now they had ended federal abortion protections. Even
with Trump out of office, Republicans were and are undermining
our democracy by eliminating the individual rights that generations of Americans died to protect. The choice facing women—
and every person in the country—has now become crystal clear.
This fight is about freedom. There can be no second-class citizens.

The clarity of the choice now facing Americans does not scare
me. It energizes me and gives me hope. As Coretta Scott King
argued, "Struggle is a never-ending process. Freedom is never
really won, you earn it and win it in every generation."[10]

It is our generation's turn to renew the struggle and earn
our freedom, as generations of Black women before us have
done. They have set an example of how we can think about this
moment. In 1989 the Supreme Court's ruling in *Webster v. Reproductive Health Services* let states impose funding restrictions on
abortions. Black women's response to it provides us with a model.
Shirley Chisholm, Donna Brazile, Eleanor Holmes Norton, Maxine Waters, Dorothy Height, Loretta Ross, and several others
released a statement entitled "We Remember: African American
Women Are for Reproductive Freedom." "Choice is the essence of
freedom," they explained. "It's what we African-Americans have
struggled for all these years."[11]

"We Remember" is a manifesto for freedom. In vivid language, it establishes Black women's experiences as essential to
understanding the connection between reproductive rights and
democratic freedom.

Five years later, in 1994, another group of Black women—
Women of African Descent for Reproductive Justice—gathered
in Chicago and went a step further. They challenged the established mainstream women's rights movement to make room for

women who did not have a seat at the table. It was here they "recognized that the women's rights movement, led by and representing middle-class and wealthy white women, could not defend the needs of women of color and other marginalized women and trans people."[12] They saw the need for their own national movement to uplift the needs of the most marginalized women, families, and communities. With this stance, they launched a movement for reproductive justice, combining demands for reproductive rights and for social justice.[13]

It's not hard to understand why Black women throughout U.S. history have so clearly seen the link between their own bodies and freedom. Each generation has helped enlarge and enrich the very meaning of freedom. As we confront today's threats to our democracy, what will our generation's contribution to the struggle and meaning of freedom be? And who will decide?

There is much to take issue with in the *Dobbs* decision. But the draft opinion by Justice Samuel Alito got at least one thing right. The decision, he wrote, "allows women on both sides of the abortion issue to seek to affect the legislative process by influencing public opinion, lobbying legislators, voting, and running for office . . . women are not without electoral or political power."[14]

This may be the one place where Black women activists and Alito are in agreement. For women to have freedom—to have control over their bodies and to be first-class citizens—we have to have political power. On this much, we agree. Women are not without electoral or political power. It's up to us to use it—a challenge we should accept.

That means we cannot be deterred by the Supreme Court's and anti-choice Republicans' decision to take away our most fundamental rights. The real path to protecting our freedom is clear. We must keep and expand our majorities from the statehouses to the halls of Congress and elect a real pro-choice majority to protect abortion rights, expand abortion access, and support equal participation in the democratic process.

And we have to do it by creating space for everyone at the table. This means building a coalition that reflects the United States—including men and women, young and old, rural and urban, Black, brown, Indigenous, immigrant, cis, and trans Americans. Teachers, bus drivers, health care providers, activists, moms, scientists, and small business owners all need to work together to make this vision a reality. And together we must engage in the political process.

Voting is one step, but we have to do more than vote. Part of building a successful movement for change is being unafraid to express our power in the halls of government. We have to be ready to run for office. We have to run and win to change the world.

Our ability to protect our rights, to win back those rights, and to ensure access to the ballot is determined by who we elect. For too long, we have all been governed by mostly wealthy, mostly white, mostly men. We all need to work to ensure that our voices are heard—and represented—in government. That means we need to elect more women. It means we need to elect more people whose lived experience is like ours. As Rep. Ayanna Pressley (D-MA) has noted, "The people closest to the pain, should be the closest to the power, driving and informing the policymaking."[15]

We can already see the impact of electing more women to public office. Being in the room matters. For example, two Black women—Rep. Alma Adams (D-NC) and Rep. Lauren Underwood (D-IL)—created the Black Maternal Health Caucus and used their power to draw attention and policy to the country's massive Black maternal health crisis. Holly J. Mitchell, who served as a California state senator from 2013 to 2020, led the fight for passage of the state's CROWN Act to ensure that Black women would not face discrimination because of their hairstyle and hair texture. And after Vice President Harris broke one of the highest glass ceilings, she became the first political leader to welcome abortion providers to the White House.

Despite the success women have had in office, we need more women at the table to create the change we seek. When Coretta Scott King told us it was up to each generation, she didn't say it would be easy. We live in an environment that isn't hospitable to women running for office. With all the firsts we've had, we still have too many firsts yet to accomplish. Only two Black women have ever been elected to the U.S. Senate, and none serve there now. And no Black woman has ever been elected governor of a state. As of this writing, the largest number of women ever to serve at once in the U.S. House of Representatives was 129 (125 voting members) in 2023. The most at once in the Senate was twenty-five in 2023 and previously in 2019. What would it mean for the United States to have women majorities in both chambers? Or to have a woman in the oval office? What if we made it happen in the next decade?

The threats we face are urgent and require larger numbers of women to take action in order to overcome them. This means we must think about scale and meet people where they are—in their communities. We must tap into the grass roots to build a pipeline that provides a steady stream of women to run for local office and beyond. We must pay attention to every race, for every office, at every level. And we must continue to expand the map so that more Democratic pro-choice women can compete for office in more states. Today's Mississippi could be the Georgia or North Carolina of tomorrow. The pendulum of freedom swings vigorously. Hamer once said, "You don't run away from problems. You just face them."[16] I believe this is true. And I believe that when you do face your problems, you change the world.

ON VOTING ACCESS

Taifa Smith Butler

"Is this your first time?" asked a poll worker.

"Yes," replied Jasmine, my nineteen-year-old daughter.

After welcoming her, the poll worker announced Jasmine's first-time status, and the polling place erupted in applause and congratulations. I beamed with pride at the simple acknowledgment of my daughter, a new voter, participating in one of the most fundamental practices of our democracy. When it was my turn to check in, I handed a poll worker my driver's license for identification purposes—muscle memory from living and voting in Georgia for the previous twenty-three years. The worker kindly explained that New Jersey did not require showing identification, eliminating an obstacle for those trying to cast a ballot.

Despite the advancements and voting rights victories of the civil rights movement, the fight to protect ballot access for all is still a critical priority for ensuring a thriving multiracial democracy. Ever since the U.S. Supreme Court's 2013 decision in *Shelby v. Holder*—eroding provisions in the 1965 Voting Rights Act that provided federal oversight and preclearance requirements for changes to state voter laws—anti-Black and antidemocratic polices have erased generations of work toward fulfilling the promises of voting rights and full citizenship.[1] The ruling has allowed for selective interpretation by the courts and a patchwork of restrictive anti-voting laws and blatant power grabs in racist redistricting processes and political gerrymandering. These practices undermine not only ballot access but also the political power of the most marginalized communities.

As my experience shows, voters face inequitable access to the ballot depending on where they live and how cumbersome or restrictive voting policies are at the state level. But this is no surprise. According to journalist Ari Berman, at times of expanded voter turnout and heightened voter engagement, states have typically responded by passing restrictive voter laws—a never-ending cycle.[2] In response to the historic turnout in the 2020 and 2022 federal elections, state legislators continue to introduce and pass restrictive laws under the guise of preventing virtually nonexistent voter fraud and alleged concerns for election security.

Increased voter turnout and engagement alone will not dismantle the power structures holding us back. It will also take more than a single election cycle—or intervention point—to shift the balance of power. To expand protections for voting rights, and to protect and bolster access to the ballot, we need to build models and systems that aim to protect rights and freedoms for all and to ensure that American democracy lives up to its ideals and its values of freedom and liberty.

Voting access has always been a starting point. It is the foundation of U.S. citizenship and a demonstration of political power. But for many, voting access remains a mere technicality on paper, as various obstacles impede free and clear access to the ballot. While some states have done a good job of protecting and expanding voting access, the disparate treatment of voting rights under the law has resulted in a tiered system of rights and access.

As fervently as many American leaders advocate for democracy abroad, so should they reflect that energy at home. The decades-long conservative political agenda to dismantle equity and deny equal rights under the law, while simultaneously consolidating wealth and power among the one percent, requires more than mere access. Our work requires us to address these inequities with solutions that will explicitly help those who have been historically excluded and marginalized from full participation in our democracy.

Creating and sustaining an inclusive democracy requires an explicit agenda with strategic interventions at both the federal and state level.[3] We could settle voter access once and for all by passing federal voting rights legislation that restores the Voting Rights Act and implements national standards for elections and ballot access, including enfranchisement for all. Expanding opportunities for enfranchisement means restoring voting rights to people affected by the racist criminal legal system. It also includes ending barriers to the ballot for those who have been detained pretrial, who retain the right to vote but are often blocked from voting. Institutional barriers leave potential eligible voters without recourse or even awareness that their rights are being denied.

Establishing an affirmative right to vote within the Constitution itself could also provide vigorous protection of voting rights that would alleviate the need for nearly constant litigation. A right-to-vote constitutional amendment would not only establish the fundamental right to vote but would also provide concrete remedies for addressing barriers to full political participation.[4]

Other possible interventions include making Election Day a national holiday, to allow more people the opportunity to vote; implementing racial equity practices; and expanding opportunities for voter registration.

In his first hundred days in office, President Joe Biden issued a visionary executive order promoting access to voting. It directed federal agencies to "consider ways to expand citizens' opportunities to register to vote and to obtain information about, and participate in, the electoral process."[5] A bold vision for action requires an equally bold commitment to implementation. State-level government agencies such as departments of motor vehicles and public assistance agencies should facilitate voter registration at points of service.

It is estimated that full implementation of the voting rights executive order could result in 3.5 million more voter registrations per year.[6] But two years after the president announced the order, the federal government has yet to tap into its full potential.[7]

Beyond policy solutions protecting and expanding the right to vote, an inclusive democracy agenda is not complete without a clear commitment to self-determination for the millions of people living in Washington, D.C., Puerto Rico, Guam, American Samoa, the U.S. Virgin Islands, and the Northern Mariana Islands.[8] As outlined in Demos's self-determination policy, "ending the centuries-long disenfranchisement of Washingtonians and the ongoing colonization of the U.S. territories is absolutely key to a fully inclusive democracy. We can do that by listening to the demands of the people of D.C. and of the territories, who want to decide their own political status."[9]

Championed by Rep. Eleanor Holmes Norton (D-DC), the U.S. House of Representatives passed H.R. 51 in 2020 and again in 2021, which set the stage for D.C. to finally achieve statehood. But the bill stalled in the Senate, a body in which D.C. residents have no representation. Abolishing the filibuster, a relic of the Jim Crow era, could provide a pathway for pro-democracy legislation to finally make its way to becoming law.[10]

Still, our efforts cannot rely on federal officials alone. We must adopt a state-by-state approach to address the patchwork of restrictive Jim Crow–era election laws by passing inclusive democracy legislation, including universal voter registration, vote by mail, same day registration, and automatic voter registration. We can create nonpartisan citizens groups such as the Georgia Peanut Gallery, which monitors the state's election system and county boards of elections to ensure fair, transparent, and accessible elections.

Without affirmative federal legislation, enfranchisement for all has been a state-by-state effort. Organizers in Florida, Louisiana, North Carolina, Minnesota, and others must fight to restore rights to millions of voters. In February 2023, Minnesota's Restore the Vote Coalition secured a major victory after state legislators passed a bill restoring voting rights to more than fifty thousand Minnesotans.[11]

It is past time for those of us who believe in freedom to reclaim that mantle from conservatives who pervert and distort concepts of freedom in efforts to repress and deny personal liberty. From abortion rights to voting rights, from restrictions on free speech to the right to protest, conservative ideologues are intent on stripping us down to the bare minimum, often removing meaningful access to the political process.

Our predecessors understood that we must leverage our collective votes to achieve significant change. Voting access without structural changes and decision makers with the political will to act will not translate into sustainable progress. As anti-lynching crusader Ida B. Wells-Barnett affirmed in her 1910 essay "How Enfranchisement Stops Lynching," ballot access is tied directly to protecting personal freedom and liberty.[12] "With no sacredness of the ballot, there can be no sacredness of human life itself," she explained. "For if the strong can take the weak man's ballot when it suits his purpose to do so, he will take his life also."

Like Wells-Barnett, I see ballot access as connected to our ability to achieve meaningful wins in the struggle for human rights. In 2022 I had the privilege of contributing to the policy pathway on voting rights and full citizenship in "An Economy for All: Building a 'Black Women Best' Legislative Agenda" from the Congressional Caucus on Black Women and Girls.[13] We envisioned the policy pathway as encompassing broader social rights like health care, housing, and childcare.

Policies that place people first require more than access to the ballot.[14] Our communities will not thrive if people are barely surviving. And beyond surviving, people deserve to live full lives, which requires the best we can offer, not the bare minimum. Connecting voting rights directly with the issues affecting people's daily lives also provides increased opportunities for converting infrequent voters and new voters like my daughter into champions of democracy.

In the voting rights and full citizenship policy pathway, we also recognized the necessity for embracing an economic democracy framework. At Demos, the think tank I lead, we focus on building governing power for the *demos*, the people. And we see our democracy and our economy as one.

One of the hallmarks of an economic democracy is co-governance, providing opportunities for everyday people to become a part of the institutions that govern our lives. The Texas Organizing Project (TOP), one of our state-level inclusive democracy movement partners, is leading the way in co-governance innovations. In the aftermath of Hurricane Harvey, TOP organizers worked alongside community members in Harris County to address inequities in resource allocation and disaster relief.[15] Through a combination of voter turnout in a county election and increasing resident leadership within local governance bodies, TOP has created opportunities for accountability and provided space for people to be directly involved in making decisions impacting their communities.

In addition to bolstering community leadership through co-governance, investing in a small donor democracy can help unstack the deck and combat a system that allows corporations and wealthy white individuals to determine who gets to run for office and how decisions are made.[16] During the 2022 midterm election cycle, wealthy donors such as Dick Uihlein and Peter Thiel poured millions into campaigns, directly supporting extremist candidates and organizations funding disinformation campaigns targeted at deterring people from voting.[17] Their excessive spending in elections makes the concept of "one person, one vote" virtually nonexistent. In addition, the fear-mongering and ugly distortions of policy proposals that provide support and care for marginalized communities, including transgender people, creates a false and dangerous narrative that fighting for equity and the rights of marginalized people somehow harms other Americans.

Even as we are fighting to protect and expand voting rights, we must also protect our wins. And once we achieve a win, safeguarding its advancements helps to ensure that our progress will not be impeded by right-wing extremists who work to suppress the vote and silence the voices of Black and brown people. Once we eliminate all the barriers of voter registration and secure smooth and equitable access to the ballot for all, we can engage in much more transformative ways to strengthen our democracy.

It is easy to say that elections may have consequences, but the greatest consequence remains the failure to invest in sustained year-round engagement and institutional support for building an inclusive democracy that works for all. Sustained engagement and support are needed to welcome new voters like my daughter Jasmine who are taking their first steps toward becoming stewards of democracy.

ON REPARATIONS

Hon. Sheila Jackson Lee

Black women in the United States experience myriad obstacles to our success. As women, we face sexism, misogyny, glass ceilings, and gender stereotypes aimed at thwarting our ambitions. And as Black people, we face overt racism, unconscious bias, discrimination, and racial stereotypes aimed at excluding us from leadership roles. Black women are at the intersection of these two sets of barriers. These daunting forces are designed to deny us a seat at the table of a truly inclusive democracy in America.

And yet, we persist. We succeed. We still take our seat at the table.

When young Black women ask me how I overcame those obstacles and what advice I have to help them succeed, I generally emphasize several key points: know your community's history; identify your goals and be committed to achieving them; develop a tangible roadmap of strategies and tactics to achieve your goals; stay focused on your ambitions and do not allow challenges to dissipate your motivation; never allow naysayers to deter you from your ambitions but instead transform their venom into your fuel; collaborate with others who share your values or want you to be successful; expand your networks by becoming involved in groups that do good work; and always persist with resilience, and when you think you've hit a wall, persist still further.

These lessons helped me access the opportunities that were presented to me over the years. They also enabled me to create opportunities when none were apparent. I drew inspiration from Black women of the past as well as from others I observed while growing up. These women did not have an abundance of opportunities, and they were not welcomed onto a fast track toward success. Instead, they created their own success—gaining inclusion in society and in our democracy—through focus, persistence, resilience, and indefatigable dedication, aided by their communities and networks. I draw on these models today as I fight for truth, facts, reconciliation, and reparations for Black Americans.

For centuries in the United States, Black people were relegated to second-class status. We suffered indignities and trauma from denigration by governmental edicts and the societal enactment of those policies. The imprimatur of official authority legalized the domination of Black people by whites under the system of slavery. And in its aftermath, new laws perpetuated the malfeasance and exacerbated the vile and inhumane treatment thrust upon us.

To recognize the changes that are needed today, we must first reflect on the past. During the colonial period, African Americans had no rights, freedoms, or protections. Our nation's founding documents did no better. Even the inspiring and visionary wisdom of the Declaration of Independence ignored women by stating that "all men are created equal," when it could easily have recognized the equality of all *people*. The most grievous scar on our otherwise beloved U.S. Constitution was the "three-fifths compromise" in which the humanity of African Americans was diminished by assessing our value as merely three-fifths of a person when determining a state's population for legislative representation.

In subsequent years, various laws and policies, including the Slave Codes, the Missouri Compromise, the Fugitive Slave Laws, the Kansas-Nebraska Act, and the *Dred Scott* decision upheld racial injustices in the United States. For much of American history, African Americans could not even imagine being part of an inclusive democracy. They hardly had a chance to elevate themselves or their children through education, improved quality of life, financial accretion, or the transfer of generational wealth.

The modern civil rights movement ushered in a new era of inclusive democracy, rights, freedoms, and opportunities for Black Americans. The most consequential laws of the period include the 1964 Civil Rights Act, the 1965 Voting Rights Act, and the 1968 Civil Rights Act, which included the Fair Housing Act. Without these laws instituting fairness, providing justice, and prohibiting rampant discrimination, American society would not have achieved the gains that today we regard as essential and irrevocable.

As a member of the U.S. House of Representatives, I recognize that I am a beneficiary of the relatively recent gains of the civil rights movement. I was part of the first Yale Law School graduating class that included women, and I have served in Congress since January 3, 1995. My career has coincided with landmark growth in the number of African American women who have reached this high echelon.

At the same time, I frequently reflect on the history from which I have been elevated, the shoulders on which I stand, and the sacrifices that generations of Black women suffered so that Black women might gain our rightful place in American society and government today. I am always mindful of the great responsibility I bear to represent the countless African American women who have been dismissed, ignored, vilified, excluded, and even tormented throughout American history.

We continue to face steep challenges. Some may suggest that racism, sexism, and misogyny stem from social tensions that are endemic to our society, and that they have never abated. But we have made meaningful progress in combating these evils. Today the arc of societal justice trends toward the expansion of rights and respect for all.

In recent years, several factors have threatened this progress—especially the election of Donald Trump to the highest office in the nation. Trump's racist, sexist, misogynistic, and xenophobic comments and policies gave license to his supporters to publicly express those same horrendous views. Trump—who referred to African nations and Haiti as "shithole countries"—routinely hurled harsh attacks against African American women, including journalists Yamiche Alcindor, Abby Phillip, and April Ryan, Vice President Kamala Harris, former Georgia gubernatorial candidate Stacey Abrams, Rep. Maxine Waters (D-CA), Washington, D.C., mayor Muriel Bowser, New York attorney general Letitia James, and Trump's former assistant Omarosa Manigault Newman.[1] He even lambasted Black women who as civil servants helped to count ballots in the 2020 election.[2] It's hard to ignore the links between his antipathy for Black women and the January 6 insurrection that he orchestrated, as well as the rise in domestic extremism.

This form of white supremacy has long roots. Iconic Black intellectual W. E. B. Du Bois wrote in *Black Reconstruction in America*:

The white group of laborers, while they received a low wage, were compensated in part by a sort of public and psychological wage. They were given public deference and titles of courtesy because they were white. They were admitted freely with all classes of white people to public functions, public parks, and the best schools. The police were drawn from their ranks, and the courts, dependent on their votes, treated them with such leniency as to encourage lawlessness.[3]

This mindset, and the acts it motivates, make a compelling case for taking action to blunt racism and misogyny by changing hearts and minds with facts, truth, and reconciliation. Only by facing our country's history head on and by offering solutions that address long-festering problems can our nation truly heal. A more inclusive democracy requires that we establish the truth, inject it into the public consciousness, and use it as the basis for an expansion of rights, freedoms, and protections for all Americans.

One of the first steps to realizing this goal is extending reparations to Black Americans. The legendary congressman John Conyers (D-MI), a founder of the Congressional Black Caucus, first introduced H.R. 40 in 1989. I reintroduced it in Congress in 2021.[4] I had returned to it in recent years in order to facilitate tangible, meaningful, long-term solutions to the economic disparity in this country. H.R. 40 pays homage to "40 acres and a mule"—the federal government's promise of reparations to the formerly enslaved in the aftermath of the Civil War. H.R. 40 provides justice, equity, truth, and accountability.

H.R. 40 has a three-part strategy. First, it calls for a factual, historical account of African Americans' plight during the eras of slavery, legalized violence, government racism, Jim Crow, exclusion, discrimination, and inequality. This truthful narrative will expose the fallacies of revisionism and misinformation, which have become favorite tools of those with racist motives and agendas. The bill asserts that Black history *is* American history.

Second, it calls for a national apology to be given for government actions that legalized oppression, violence, inequality, and exclusion from the means of socioeconomic mobility and generational wealth. Reconciliation requires an apology that acknowledges the government's collusion with white supremacy in past eras. This will provide accountability for past wrongs, heal the national soul, and confer official vindication upon its victims. Without an apology, there can be no closure or justice for our ancestors who suffered hideous torment.

Third, H.R. 40 will help generate new ideas about what can be done to right past wrongs. It creates a national commission to examine slavery and discrimination from 1619 to the present and to recommend appropriate remedies. The commission would identify past federal and state government support for the institution of slavery, discrimination in the public and private sectors against freed slaves and their descendants, and lingering effects of slavery that affect African Americans and the nation today.

Reparations are necessary to advance equity and create a level playing field for African Americans who are still disadvantaged by the indignities of previous eras. Rather than simply extending payments to individuals, making reparations would be far more expansive. It would focus on providing remedies in multiple forms to equitably address the varied kinds of disadvantages Black people sustained from chattel slavery and its ongoing vestiges. These forms of repair include providing enhanced aid for parents of pre-K children, best-of-class educational and afterschool programs, tuition-free college education, reduced rate home loans and insurance, and loan guarantees for Black-owned start-up businesses.

Reparations would redress the long, despicable history of racist laws. The Slave Codes of colonial days, the U.S. Constitution's "three-fifths compromise," the Fugitive Slave Act of 1850, *Plessy v. Ferguson*—among others—institutionalized blatant racism into our country's legal framework. This contemptible trend continued as repeated efforts to pass a law criminalizing lynching in the United States failed for over a century.[5]

These policies prevented African Americans from gaining a toehold—let alone a foothold—for success. American laws inhibited the social and physical mobility of Black people. They limited access to education and therefore to wealth and other opportunities for self-improvement and uplift. They kept Black women from achieving aspirations beyond raising children and working in the fields. They kept our ancestors in a perpetual state of anxiety and ill health, so much so that civil rights activist Fannie Lou Hamer declared, "I'm sick and tired of being sick and tired."[6]

The laws emanating from the civil rights movement prohibited the most racist practices that subjugated African Americans. However, they did not result in full reconciliation with American society. Racial inequality persisted long after the movement ended, leaving the nation vulnerable to the problems that continue to generate division, racial disparities, and injustice. Moreover, the civil rights movement did not resolve the matter of economic inequality: African Americans still lag far behind their peers in the accumulation of wealth.[7]

H.R. 40 will help to move the nation forward by advancing the urgent need for reparations and restorative justice. It will help facilitate a national reckoning to make America a "more perfect union." By establishing the truth through telling the factual, accurate history of Black Americans, it can allow our nation to begin to honestly confront its ignominious racial history. Acknowledging this history will help all Americans recognize the need for genuine reconciliation and economic redress. By providing an official national apology for the government's role in perpetuating past tragedies and current inequities, H.R. 40 can enable the nation to begin to heal, and African Americans will recognize a genuine commitment on the part of the nation's leaders to embark on a new era of true diversity, equity, and inclusion. By establishing a national commission composed of thoughtful academics and experts from various backgrounds to study reparations and make tangible recommendations, it will permit the nation to move one step closer toward realizing the ideals of American democracy. Only then can we build a nation on justice and equality through, as President Abraham Lincoln said in the Gettysburg Address, a "government of the people, by the people, and for the people."

Black women have emerged from centuries of mistreatment and subjugation to become among the most effective activists and advocates for diversity, equity, and inclusion. With increasing frequency, we ascend to leadership roles in an effort to right the wrongs of the past and institute an equitable society. Our dedication to inclusive democracy, and the fortitude with which we pursue it, compels reciprocation in the form of official government action that reflects the travails we have endured to reach this point.

By passing H.R. 40, Congress can initiate the national reckoning that we need to bridge racial divides. And this is the time to do it. We must seize the opportunity by instituting the reparations commission and H.R. 40's other components. Whether they are initiated by statute or by executive action, the establishment of a factually accurate historical record, the issuance of an official acknowledgment of the government's role in that history, and the creation of a commission that develops proposals for reparations are all vital steps. They will enable our country to come to terms with the past while ushering in a new era of public trust and national unity. They will help us move closer toward a shared vision that lives up to the promise laid forth in our founding documents. Reparations for Black people would advance respect and reconciliation—and the hope that one day all Americans can walk together toward a more inclusive and just future.

ON DISABILITY AND THE AMERICAN DREAM

Andraéa LaVant

As a teenager, I had no activity that I loathed more than riding the city bus. Growing up in Louisville, Kentucky, during the 1990s in a middle-class Black family, I was accustomed to being chauffeured everywhere by my parents. While we were not rich—my father was a college-turned-nonprofit-administrator and my mother was a banking professional—our Toyotas, Nissans, Volvos, and even our massive Dodge Ram van got us from place to place. Thus, when the time came for me to navigate the city bus, I was incredibly embarrassed. But not for reasons most people would imagine.

I was diagnosed with spinal muscular atrophy (SMA), a form of muscular dystrophy, when I was just shy of two years old. My mother began to notice distinctions between my physical development and that of her peers' children. I was unable to walk without assistance. I was unable to pull myself up in my crib. Ultimately, my parents' concern led to a diagnosis of a neuro-muscular condition that would impact my full muscle function and all my daily activities. I would eventually reach a time when I was unable to walk. At age two, I began to wear leg braces, and a year later I started using a walker. By the time I was seven, I was rolling around in a hot pink manual wheelchair. By seventeen, my disability had progressed to a point where I required assistance with everything from getting out of bed to bathing to using the restroom.

While I adjusted to these changes, I was also finding my way academically. As a student, I thrived in the classroom, and upon graduating from high school, I headed to Tennessee to attend college. The summer before I left, my dad helped me land an administrative assistant job at the local housing authority. Although my parents had by then divorced, together they had managed to accommodate my school, church, and extracurricular schedule such that my inability to drive didn't seem to impact me deeply. However, our newly conflicting work schedules meant that for the first time in my life, I'd have to learn to ride the city bus.

Even though, for the first few trips on the bus, my mom traveled with me, I could literally feel my heart beating in my throat. I hated the idea that people were staring at me, and that the bus driver and passengers were inconvenienced while I rolled my power wheelchair onto the lift and tried to maneuver without rolling over anyone's feet. I especially hated having to make someone relinquish their seat so that I could have space to ride the bus. While I deeply respected my ancestors who had fought tirelessly, and even lost their lives, so that those who bore the same skin color as mine could sit wherever they wanted to on the bus, I didn't consider myself in the same category as they were. I was Black *and* disabled, and I didn't see myself as worthy to take up that much space on the bus—or anywhere else, for that matter.

Less than a decade after my bus riding shame emerged, my educational and career path led me to a dream job in Washington, D.C. By then, I had bigger concerns than riding the bus. My disability-related needs had expanded. I still needed someone to get me out of bed—not to get to school anymore but to go to work to pay my bills. And I needed someone to help me at home. I also needed quality health care, including an accessible doctor's office and professionals who would actually listen to me.

These were just some of my needs, and they were only a small fraction of the issues that my disabled comrades, particularly disabled people of color, were facing. While I initially had no knowledge of the Americans with Disabilities Act (ADA) of 1990, I began to study the law intently as part of my professional endeavors.[1] When I became a youth development specialist for a national nonprofit working with disabled youth, I kept flashcards of the five titles of the ADA—Employment, Public Services, Public Accommodations, Telecommunications, and Miscellaneous—so I could reference the law in conversations as needed.

My work and lived experiences in D.C. and other parts of the country proved to me that the ADA was simply a baseline. It created a bare minimum that provided disabled people with rights to access certain things. But rights that are achieved without mindset shifts and without consideration of race, class, sexual/gender identity, and other social categories are ultimately ineffective. While I remain grateful to those who fought to establish these rights, it didn't take me long to understand that rights do not ensure an inclusive democracy. For me as a Black, disabled, and queer woman, rights are not enough.

There are disproportionate connections between disability and other cultural identities and experiences that deeply impact the ways disabled Americans live. Overlapping systems of oppression, including racism, ableism, and sexism, keep disabled people, especially disabled people of color, from experiencing true liberation. When I envision a truly inclusive democracy, it is in consideration of these intersecting identities and in opposition to the systems and structures that continue to inhibit our freedom.

My experiences and those of my parents underscore how these systems work in tandem to limit opportunities and access for disabled Americans of color. My parents were educated in an era preceding the Individuals with Disabilities Education Act (IDEA) of 1975, which entitles everyone a free and appropriate public education regardless of disability status. When it came time to enroll me in elementary school, my mother inquired about "special needs" schools for her disabled daughter. The school's administrator then determined my physical disability did not require the support that special needs classes provided. Because of the vigilance of this school administrator, my needs were not misidentified, and I had a mainstream educational experience, an opportunity that many disabled people of color do not have.

Historically, Black and brown children are more likely than others to be misdiagnosed with disabilities, landing them in overcrowded and understaffed special education classrooms where they do not belong.[2] Others are mislabeled "troublesome," "deviant," or "bad" and are ultimately suspended or expelled. These experiences of oppression significantly impact their access to the education that can lead to higher education and gainful employment opportunities, which in turn has an impact on their economic standing. Even when children of color with disabilities are diagnosed properly, they often are not given appropriate services and treatments to support their academic success.

The challenges that disabled Americans of color face extend to the health care system. Since the founding of this nation, disabled people's bodies have been deemed inhuman, broken, not valuable, and all too often disposable. As such, the system supposedly designed to care for the well-being of humanity has continuously failed us. From sterilization and the lack of long-term health care planning to minimal mental health services and poor personal care services, the U.S. health care system is one of the most oppressive that disabled Americans must contend with. For those like me who experience multiple forms of oppression as a Black, disabled, and queer woman, disparate treatment runs even deeper. Barriers include everything from lack of access to physically accessible facilities and equipment to lack of communication access such as interpreters, Braille, and large print.

Threats to quality health care currently present themselves in myriad ways. In recent years, Americans have been combating debt ceilings that disrupt various federal benefit programs, overall cuts to Medicaid and Medicare, a lack of affordable health care, low wages for home care workers, and so much more. As someone who relies on daily personal care services for all general activities of daily living, including dressing, bathing, and grooming, I have found myself at the forefront of the affordable care and home- and community-based services (HCBS) debates. I have testified before government officials; I have offered commentary on local and national news programs; and I have protested on Capitol Hill. I even had to plead with my local congressperson and crowdfund to gain resources to pay for my personal care services so I could stay in my home rather than live in a nursing home. I have had to take these steps even after working so hard to achieve what I had been told was the American dream.

For disabled Americans—and especially disabled Americans of color, women, and those who are queer—the American dream is elusive. Much work remains to be done to build an inclusive democracy that attends to the needs of all Americans, including those who are most marginalized in society. A truly inclusive democracy would realize, for all Americans, true liberation from all forms of oppression, including systemic, institutional, interpersonal, and even internalized oppressive constructs. While describing a picture of this ideal world would be delightful, today's societal climate suggests it would seem an "impossible dream."

We may never reach all our goals, but this does not mean that we cannot work toward this aspiration. I believe we can take some concrete steps to eliminate some of these constructs. First, we need to redefine disability. Current views of disability, from both policy and cultural perspectives, are outdated. The ADA, for example, defines disability as "a physical or mental impairment that substantially limits one or more major life activities" or a condition of "being regarded as having such an impairment." This definition has provided the definitive view of disability in relation to policy, yet it is challenged in its singular view of disabled people. In order to influence both policy and culture, decision makers and policy makers must expand the definition of disability to consider the societal structures that impact and even oppress disabled people, especially people of color, women, and queer Americans.

New legislation for people with disabilities would be required to accompany this change. Such landmark legislation would consider the structures that uphold ableism and the overlapping systems of oppression. It would include expanded funding and requirements in relation to health care, education access, the democratic process (voting rights), housing, gender equity, environment and climate, decriminalization, and more.

Moreover, we need to work toward increasing the representation of marginalized individuals and communities, including disabled people, in positions of leadership and power. This includes all sectors of society such as public policy, entertainment, technology, and financial services. These changes will serve as a telltale sign of the shift of our democracy toward inclusion. To supply this increased representation, we must build a sustainable pipeline of qualified individuals who have the education, skills, and experience required to hold positions of power at every decision-making table. This means we must have programs and laws that provide access to higher education, offer quality employment opportunities, and protect against discrimination to ensure the successful advancement of marginalized Americans.

Over twenty years have passed since my bus riding days. Now when I wait at a bus stop, I do so with pride—but also some sadness. I stick my neck out and hold my head high, smiling widely as the ramp flips out like a red carpet to invite me on board. I take my time rolling to the seat designated for me, refusing to apologize to disgruntled drivers who think I'm holding up their route, or to passengers who have to move their belongings so I can take up space. I think of the wheelchair users and other disabled folks of the 1970s and '80s who barricaded major city streets and chained themselves to buses so that I can ride the bus whenever I please. I am grateful for the right I have to ride public transportation.

Yet every time I arrive at my seat, I consider my countless disabled kin who are still dreaming about riding the bus. Some disabled community members live in rural communities without bus routes, or are unable to afford bus fare, or are unable to access care and support services to help them leave the house. These people are at the forefront of my mind when I dream of an inclusive democracy. And until we all get there, I'll forge ahead in solidarity with my comrades in this fight toward the realization of that dream.

ON REPRODUCTIVE RIGHTS

Atima Omara

> We hold these truths to be self-evident, that all men are created equal, that they are endowed by their Creator with certain unalienable rights, that among these are life, liberty and the pursuit of happiness.
>
> —*Declaration of Independence, 1776*

The wealthy, landowning white men who co-signed the Declaration of Independence in protest of their tyrannical king deeply believed that they possessed unalienable rights. However, they did not believe these rights extended to white women, Black people, or Indigenous people. The signers did not envision a nation for people like me. Regardless, I believe that unalienable rights extend to everyone. That is the essence of human rights, and they are a fundamental element of an inclusive democracy.

When I served in student government in college, I remember meeting a foreign exchange student from Sweden who also participated in his university's student government. During our conversations, he asked me and one of my classmates about the U.S. government. At some point, the topic turned to the overrepresentation of men in positions of power, particularly white men in the U.S. Congress. To this day, I still remember his reaction. "My God! How is your government even legal?!" he exclaimed. Some of Sweden's political parties had quotas to ensure gender representation. It was the first time I had heard someone question the U.S. political system in that way.

Since then I have helped those underrepresented in our government—including women, people of color, youth, disabled, and LGBTQ+ people—get elected to office. I have even run for public office. Though we have made inroads at the local, state, and federal levels, we are still far from having a government that reflects the population. Unlike Sweden, the United States does not have any quotas. Over the last few centuries, most of the laws that emerged from our representative government have not captured the needs of its ever-changing population—with the exception of white men. It is not surprising that a government led primarily by white men has continually failed to consider reproductive rights as an unalienable right.

The most marginalized Americans—women of color and disabled people—were most impacted by this control. White doctors often described enslaved Black women as "breeders." One judge in South Carolina ruled that enslaved Black people had no legal claims on their children. After his presidency, Andrew Jackson recommended that troops kill Indigenous women and children to complete the extermination of Native peoples. Reproductive coercion also found its way into late-nineteenth-century immigration policies, such as the plan to make it more difficult for Asian women to enter the country, as a form of population control. By the early twentieth century, many women of color were victims of involuntary sterilization as well as medical testing involving unsafe contraception. Those who had children lived in constant fear that the state would take them away.[1] Federal and state laws also targeted disabled people—enabling the sterilization of disabled people, removing their own children from their care, and upholding conservatorships that stripped the disabled of bodily autonomy.[2]

Significant changes arrived in the 1960s and '70s with the introduction of the birth control pill and legal abortion access in some states. According to the Institute for Women's Policy Research, the pill increased women's participation in the workforce, including in the fields of medicine and law.[3] These developments made it possible for women to have greater participation in public life, which has significant implications for our democracy.

Reproductive rights are vital to an inclusive democracy because they ensure that all members of society can fully participate— particularly women, transgender, and nonbinary Americans. The right to decide when and if to have a child is a powerful expression of autonomy.

The experiences of the women in my family made this point clear to me. My grandmothers did not attend high school because they both grew up in East Africa, at a time when young women were expected to get married during their teen years. They were valued for the dowry they would bring and the children they would bear. My grandmothers had few choices and complied with tradition—they married young and bore multiple children. But my mother, the firstborn, wanted a say in her own fate and rejected the same expectations. She dreamed of having a career in medicine to help her community.

My grandmother supported my mother's dreams. She helped persuade her husband to allow my mother to attend secondary school. At first, my mother decided she would not have children in order to pursue her dreams. Her education brought her to the United States. There she met and married my father and later changed her mind about having children. She *chose* her life partner and determined how many children she would have. Having access to reproductive rights changed the course of my mother's life.

Everything changed in the summer of 2022, when the U.S. Supreme Court overturned *Roe v. Wade*, the 1973 decision that had established the right to seek an abortion. All Americans born after 1973 have had legal access to abortion—as well as contraception—throughout their entire lives. But these rights have been slowly stripped away for decades. The overturning of *Roe v. Wade* is a wake-up call for all of us—we must work to restore and protect reproductive rights in the United States. They are fundamental rights for all citizens, and we cannot have an inclusive democracy without them.

To guarantee reproductive rights for everyone, we must be committed to reproductive justice, a critical feminist framework created by Black women abortion rights supporters and leaders.[4] Reproductive justice is based on the premise that Americans have the right to have a child, the right *not* to have a child, and the right to parent a child in safe and healthy environments. It provides a framework on which an inclusive democracy can be built.

Pursuing reproductive justice begins first and foremost with repealing abortion bans throughout the country. The Hyde Amendment, for example, blocks all federally funded insurance from covering the cost of abortions except in the cases of rape, incest, and life of the parent. The Hyde Amendment was initially applied to lower-income individuals who received Medicaid insurance but has since been used as a model to apply to other federally funded insurance.[5] It is just one of many abortion bans that are now used to deny care to pregnant people, especially people of color.

Abortion bans specifically target the reproductive rights of those who have limited financial resources, and they create additional challenges for those in rural areas. With miles to drive to receive even basic medical services—let alone an abortion—those who live in rural parts of the country often bear the brunt of these restrictive policies.

Ensuring that all Americans have access to safe abortions—regardless of economic status and geographic location—is part of the fight for a more inclusive democracy. We also need to preserve and expand access to contraception and to affordable reproductive health care services in general. Everyone has the right to know and understand their reproductive health and to make the right decisions for their care, regardless of their background or status.

Those who decide to have a child should have access to quality and affordable services to ensure a safe and healthy pregnancy and delivery. The United States has one of the highest rates of maternal mortality among wealthy nations, and there are wide racial disparities in *who* dies. According to the Centers for Disease Control and Prevention, "Black women are three times more likely to die from a pregnancy-related cause than White women in the United States."[6]

For many, being pregnant and raising a child is intertwined with needs for financial stability and solvency. One aspect of reproductive justice is to provide a safe and healthy environment for a child. Research has shown that being denied an abortion lowers a woman's credit score, increases her amount of debt, and makes bankruptcies and evictions more likely.[7] The social cost of being pregnant, giving birth, and raising an infant is high in a country where paid family leave, paid sick days, and affordable childcare do not exist except in a patchwork system that varies by state and job. We need a federal paid family leave plan for at least three months. As a country, we should mandate paid sick days for everyone. And we must invest in accessible, quality, and affordable childcare for the benefit of both today's parents and future generations.

We also should aim to improve the social conditions in which parents raise their children. In the United States, the simple act of going to a school, a grocery store, a mall, or a theater can mean death by a random mass shooter. Since the 1999 Columbine High School shooting, federal and state legislators have passed few laws restricting access to guns. We have a long way to go.

Raising a child in a healthy and safe environment also means prioritizing environmental justice—fighting climate change and ensuring that all Americans, regardless of where they live, have access to clean air and clean water. It requires that a person born with a disability can still live a complete and fulfilling life with access to quality care and without being forced into poverty or becoming a ward of the state. Creating a healthy and safe environment for raising children also means ensuring that every job for parents pays a livable wage.

We must be vigilant on the electoral and advocacy front as well. We must elect more politicians who are not only pro-choice but are also committed to using their power to protect and expand reproductive rights for all. This fight should be a nonpartisan issue, but those who oppose reproductive rights have weaponized the political process to block us from accessing those rights. Therefore we must engage in the political system to enshrine reproductive rights for everyone and thereby build an inclusive democracy. And I believe we can win this fight. Despite voter suppression and partisan gerrymandering, voters in the 2022 midterm elections sent a clear message: they turned out in massive numbers to support pro-choice candidates and to defeat ballot initiatives that would have banned abortion.

We must find and support candidates who reflect the diversity of our communities. We must elect those who prioritize a comprehensive progressive agenda that includes reproductive rights. In the absence of such individuals, those of us who are committed to protecting reproductive rights should strongly consider running for office. As we look to the future, we must commit ourselves to supporting these rights if we hope to build the kind of nation that would benefit us all.

ON RACE AND DISABILITY

Vilissa Thompson

In college, I completed a minor in African American studies because I wanted to deepen my knowledge of Black history and go beyond the well-known figures and events we generally discuss during February of each year. I thought I gained a firm grasp of Black history, but when I began my activist work in 2013, I spotted a glaring omission in my studies: the lives and experiences of Black disabled people in the United States.

This omission not only erases this group of Black people from U.S. history but also fails to tell the full story of the Black disabled experience. The historical contributions of Black disabled people are largely unknown, which leaves a sizable hole that needs to be filled. It also makes Black disabled people today wonder, "Have others like me ever done anything worthwhile to record or to notice?" The answer is a resounding yes! Abolitionist Harriet Tubman, civil rights activist Fannie Lou Hamer, and author Eliza Suggs are three Black disabled people who made tremendous strides in the fight for disability rights as well as the struggle for Black liberation.[1]

Black disability history is erased not only from Black history but also from disability rights history and from U.S. history in general. This is not shocking to those of us who have had to conduct our own research to uncover this history, often relying on technology and sources outside academic scholarship. The names, stories, and legacies of Black disabled people have been overlooked for far too long. I am committed to ensuring that they are no longer sidelined. They must be placed front and center in our history. We need to include these stories if we desire to build an inclusive democracy that allows all Americans, including Black disabled people, to thrive.

The marginalization of Black disabled people in American history is tied directly to the history of enslavement. As historian Jenifer L. Barclay explains, white enslavers viewed disabled enslaved people as an economic liability. Enslavers believed the disabled individual was a worthless "product," one that they could not financially exploit. However, some white enslavers did figure out a means of exploitation: if an enslaver considered the disabled person "exceptional," they sold them off to be displayed.[2] During the nineteenth century, a white enslaver sold conjoined twins Millie and Christine McKoy, known as the "Carolina Twins," for $1,000 to a showman who hired them out to tours across the country.[3] The McKoys were just two of many Black disabled people who were exploited for profit under the dehumanizing system of slavery.

Such exploitation did not stop with the legal end of slavery in 1865. It still occurs today. The interconnection between racism and ableism—the social prejudice against disabled people—has significantly reduced the opportunities and overall quality of life for Black disabled Americans. As I outlined on May 24, 2022, in my written testimony to the House Committee on Financial Services' Subcommittee on Diversity and Inclusion, disabled workers in the United States in 2020 were paid 74 cents for every dollar paid to nondisabled workers. According to the Century Foundation and the Center for Economic and Policy Research, the gap is even wider when race is added into the mix—Black disabled workers who worked full time were paid just 68 cents on average for every dollar paid to their white nondisabled counterparts.[4] In the housing sector, race and disability collide to make the realities even bleaker for Black and Hispanic renters, who are likely to experience housing discrimination at higher rates than their white counterparts.[5] And disabled people make up an estimated 50 percent of Americans killed by police.[6]

These are just a few of the startling statistics that spotlight the real consequences of the unjust systems and discrimination that Black disabled Americans face on a daily basis. We cannot begin to tackle the depths of racism and ableism in the United States without fully acknowledging the plight of Black disabled people.

Ignorance of the plight of Black disabled people affects how those in our community are able to connect to one another, both online and offline. In May 2016, I created the hashtag #DisabilityTooWhite, one of the first disability-centered hashtags on Twitter, and it quickly went viral.[7] #DisabilityTooWhite conceptualizes the exclusion, erasure, and othering of disabled people of color within and outside disability spaces. The hashtag was embraced by disabled people of color but was widely resisted by white disabled people. For twenty-four hours on Twitter, many white disabled people called me the N-word out of frustration that I had the audacity to center race in public conversations about disability.

The reluctance to center race—or other identities—is commonplace in the disability community. White disabled leaders have a long history of excluding disabled people of color, and it is not uncommon in these spaces to hear the assertion that "race is a distraction" from disability rights. The disability rights movement's overt refusal to grapple with the intersection of race and disability has led to distrust and reduced the involvement of Black disabled people in the movement, while also making room for anti-Blackness.

Some non-Black disabled people of color are also guilty of these practices. They too commit acts of violence and harm against Black disabled people, attempting to gain a semblance of power by aligning themselves with whiteness. This behavior has led to distrust, and it has decreased solidarity between disabled Black and non-Black people of color.

While the isolation of being Black and disabled is profound, both in the real world and in activist spaces, technology and social media have helped to bring Black disabled people together. We are now able to build community in ways that go beyond what we had thought possible. Technology also forces the collective disability community to have difficult and honest conversations about the wrongs committed within the disability rights movement. As Black disabled people, we no longer have to "wait" to be seen or heard by those who refuse to acknowledge our existence; we now have our own platforms to tell our truths on our terms, regardless of what others think. The power of technology to allow us to retell our history in a more intersectional and inclusive way is a true marker of the way disability activism has developed in the twenty-first century.

At the core of my activist work is a recognition that Black liberation is not possible without Black disabled people. This is an important reminder because Black communities are not always havens for us. For many, in fact, they have been spaces of harm. While some may find it difficult to accept, the reality is that Black people can be ableist in the way we treat, discuss, and engage disabled people. Even in the most progressive Black spaces, it is not uncommon to see Black disabled people completely left out of discussions. We often discuss the high Black maternal mortality rate, but we fail to consider the plight of Black disabled mothers.[8] In this country, being a disabled parent means that your rights to parent can be questioned or taken away altogether simply because you are disabled—without any proof of endangerment or neglect. Black disabled parents are fully aware that child protective services and the medical community have long histories of discrimination. The glaring absence of Black disabled people from public discussions of social issues that affect Black people means that as a society we are not addressing the needs and concerns of *all* Black people.

The discrimination, harm, and abuse that we have experienced over centuries are interwoven into the very fabric of this nation. The cousins of white supremacy—ableism, anti-Blackness, and misogynoir—are in cahoots in our psyche, our language, and our interactions. So what would an inclusive democracy look like for Black disabled people in America? The first step toward progress is for all Americans to recognize the issues that Black disabled people have and to interrogate their own thinking and actions, especially when they may cause harm to others.

Responsibility and accountability—the driving forces for creating a more inclusive democracy—can happen only with full acknowledgment of the historical experiences, triumphs, and current realities of Black disabled people. The socially constructed ignorance around the many barriers Black disabled people face on a daily basis has thwarted the United States' ability to make necessary changes. We can only combat ignorance—and misinformation—when we are intentional about incorporating Black disabled people's voices and experiences into Black, disability, and general American history.

Tackling ignorance will address the erasure of Black disabled people in various sectors of society. Recognizing how historical, political, and social dysfunctions create havoc on the quality of life for Black disabled people is an important and necessary step to holding accountable those who have the power and ability to create change. For far too long, Black disabled people have shouldered the burden of educating others, creating alternatives for safety, and the like. It is time for those who have greater privilege and resources within and without the disability communities to do what is required.

A major policy debate taking place across the nation concerns economic reparations. Within it, the financial realities of Black disabled people are rarely mentioned, much less the realities of those who rely on governmental programs like Social Security and the constraints imposed on that assistance. If one goal of reparations is to distribute monetary support to descendants of enslaved people, then factoring in the needs of Black disabled people has to be part of the conversation.

We need to get rid of one of the biggest misconceptions about disability in the United States: the erroneous assumption that disabled people already have access to all the resources we need. Many Americans have no knowledge of the costs of being disabled (often referred to as the "crip tax"). During the COVID-19 pandemic, many able-bodied Americans who had little previous knowledge of these challenges received a wake-up call when they contracted the virus and discovered that the health care system is ill-equipped to meet their basic needs, let alone the specific needs of disabled people.[9] We need to all work together to demand an overhaul of this country's ailing health and welfare infrastructure.

We must eradicate the gaps in our so-called safety nets and ensure that disabled people's quality of life is not hindered due to bureaucratic red tape or the incompetence of federal and state agencies.

The lack of accessibility for disabled Americans combined with ableism makes the lives of disabled Americans much harder than they should be. Being Black and disabled, along with any other additional marginalized identities, makes this existence even more difficult because we have no safe—or even soft—space to land if we do not create it for ourselves. This is antithetical to the notion of democracy, which should provide space for all citizens—regardless of their race, gender, class, or ability.

When people ask me if I wish I were able-bodied, my answer is always the same: "It's not the disability that gives me issues—it's society's ignorance and misunderstanding of who I am before they even know my name."

I count it a privilege to be Black and disabled. This reality has shaped my perspective on life and has informed my activism. I get to be part of two vibrant communities that help sustain me. Connecting with other Black disabled people fills my cup in ways to which words cannot do justice. I carry no shame in having this identity—anything related to shame is the burden of society and those who deem my life worthless. What is shameful is how we are treated in a nation that prides itself on being a beacon of democracy—a society that promises "liberty and justice for all." The experiences of disabled Americans demonstrate how much we have fallen short as a society.

ON TRANSGENDER RIGHTS

Raquel Willis

I recently engaged in the dangerous game of discussing politics with a man. He was an Uber driver and a white, cisgender, straight immigrant from the United Kingdom. As we explored stories from his life and talked about current events, I could almost count down to the point at which we'd begin to spar. We agreed that the image and lore of the United States as the freest country in the world was at odds with its often puritanical Christian mores. But his otherwise liberal perspective fractured once he randomly mentioned transgender people's participation in sports. He told me that trans women, whom he referred to as "men," should not compete against cisgender women.

I contemplated bursting his bubble, refusing to let my eyes glaze over and take on a defeatist disposition. After all, he seemed to assume I was a cis woman and that I would agree with his perspective. But I did not, and I proceeded to tell him that I was one of those women he had just called "men." I explained that despite being assigned male at birth, I had neither the skills nor the stamina to compete with elite athletes of any gender. I then explained that governing sports agencies like the International Olympic Committee had adopted equitable, inclusive, and science-based guidelines for sports participation.[1] His views, I explained, stemmed from a long-standing white supremacist fascination with protecting white womanhood. I drew a comparison between the demonization of Black cis women athletes—like Venus and Serena Williams and Caster Semenya—and the dissection of trans athletes in the media.

When I concluded my remarks, he assured me that he "had nothing against trans people." He changed his tune once he understood that trans people are not the hypothetical beasts that conservatives had painted us out to be. Then he asked me whether it was easier being trans today than when I first began my gender transition in 2011. His inquiry was perplexing, but I had contemplated it before. I explained that my life had improved in some ways. I am now less afraid to share my authentic perspective with a stranger, for example. However, trans people in the United States still do not receive the respect and dignity we deserve, especially those of us who are also Black. The antagonism that the mere thought of trans inclusion in sports sparked in him was just one example of the challenges trans people face daily. How had this relatively liberal man been so thoroughly indoctrinated with ignorant ideas about trans people despite more visibility for the community than ever before? The short answer is that most people still don't encounter trans people in their everyday lives, so they are receptive to the dehumanizing rhetoric spewed by bigoted conservative politicians who oppose the progress that the trans community has made in the last several decades.

At the start of the 2010s, trans experiences were still considered fringe, rarely discussed in everyday life in the United States or in the media. When I first discussed my transness with my God-fearing southern mother and siblings, I had to carefully explain the differences between sex, gender identity, gender expression, and sexual orientation. Just like me, my family did not have access to the nuances of LGBTQ+ experiences. Not until Emmy Award–winning actress Laverne Cox portrayed Sophia Burset in *Orange Is the New Black* in 2013 did many Americans pay serious attention to trans people.[2] This achievement—and Cox's subsequent appearance on the cover of *Time* magazine—sparked a new era of trans visibility in the United States. A few years later the former Olympic champion Caitlyn Jenner carried the baton forward, even as she became a right-wing political darling. Then the 2018 emergence of *Pose* provided an even more expansive blueprint for centering the stories and talent of queer and trans people of color. The show boasted the largest-ever cast of LGBTQ+ people of color and an unprecedented directorial and writing team, including Janet Mock and Our Lady J. Since then more trans and nonbinary people, especially of color, have landed prime-time TV roles.[3]

Alongside the media ascent, there was a historic rise in political trans representation. In 2017 I wrote an article on the "age of trans political power" in the Condé Nast publication *them*.[4] There I reflected on the historic wins of Virginia's Danica Roem and Minnesota's Andrea Jenkins and Phillipe Cunningham. Roem had just become the first openly trans person to be elected and to serve in any U.S. state legislature. Jenkins and Cunningham had recently joined the Minneapolis City Council as, respectively, the first openly trans Black woman and the first openly trans man of color, to be elected to public office in U.S. history.

Ahead of the 2020 election, presidential hopefuls courted

Black trans women, recognizing that support for issues impacting us signaled progressivism to a wider audience. These candidates hoped to capitalize on the massive social media platforms and widespread influence of Black trans women. Several of them reached out to me and attempted to secure endorsements from Ashlee Marie Preston and Angelica Ross. During the election season, the latter became the first trans person to host a presidential forum. Several other "firsts" followed from that election: Delawarean Sarah McBride became the first openly trans state senator in U.S. history, Taylor Small became the first openly trans representative in Vermont, Stephanie Byers became the first in Kansas, and Brianna Titone became the first in Colorado. Lisa Bunker, a transgender state legislator, was reelected in New Hampshire, and Mauree Turner became the first nonbinary state legislator in Oklahoma.[5] By 2022, these developments had seemingly resulted in an uptick in LGBTQ+ identification by members of Generation Z, those born between 1997 and 2003.[6] But there remained a grisly underbelly to the American trans experience.

Despite increased trans visibility in media and politics as well as the legalization of marriage equality, conservative politicians have ramped up proposals for anti-LGBTQ+ restrictions. In 2022 nearly three hundred pieces of legislation were introduced in states across the nation, largely focusing on trans participation in sports, trans access to health care, and LGBTQ+-conscious educational curricula.[7] The same year an *Insider* report revealed that over the previous five years, at least 175 trans people were killed domestically. Nearly two-thirds of the victims were Black, and most of the murder suspects were Black cis men.[8] This deadly culture, however, is not the result solely of the last twelve years of momentum.

The current trans political landscape has largely been shaped by early LGBTQ+ struggles occurring just after the 1969 Stonewall Riots in New York. That seismic uprising, led by a gender-diverse, multiracial collective, laid the foundation for a more visible community. In the early 1970s, Minnesota-based activist Stephen Endean pioneered gay and lesbian political lobbying. He became instrumental in pushing for Minneapolis to become one of the first major U.S. cities to pass an antidiscrimination ordinance, including sexual orientation. At the same time, he staunchly opposed the right of "transvestites" to fully dress per their identity at work. He also dismissed other activists' concerns about the need to expand public accommodations and services for LGBTQ+ people.[9]

Despite becoming a prominent figure in the post-Stonewall era, Endean rejected queer and trans militancy politics. In his posthumous 1993 memoir, *Into the Mainstream: A First-Hand Account of Twenty Years' Progress on Lesbian/Gay Rights*, he detailed how, in his Minneapolis days, he exploited respectability (and transphobia) to recruit affluent cis gay people to support his political work.[10] By 1978, his efforts helped him become the director of the Gay Rights National Lobby, and in the 1980s, he played a pivotal role in establishing the Human Rights Campaign Fund, for which he served as the group's first treasurer. In 1985, the two organizations merged to form the Human Rights Campaign (HRC), the leading face of LGBTQ+ political power in the country.

While the nascent, mostly white LGBTQ+ political scene broke ground in the 1970s, lesbian and queer cis women were often at odds with mainstream feminist movements and were combating culture wars that would inspire future conservative arguments around the professed goals of the Left. Janice Raymond would emerge as a leading figure against trans women's inclusion and existence after the 1979 release of her book *The Transsexual Empire: The Making of the She-Male*.[11] The book became a cornerstone of trans-exclusionary radical feminism and impacted the U.S. government's assessment of gender-affirming care for decades.

The civil rights and Black Power movements had no shortage of Black cis lesbian and gay voices, yet mainstream organizations often sidelined their contributions. Bayard Rustin, architect of the 1963 March on Washington for Jobs and Freedom, was often excluded by his peers. Perhaps the most noted gay figure of the civil rights movement, Bayard became more outspoken about his identity in the 1980s but maintained that it had not "greatly influenced" his role as an activist.[12] Black cis lesbians like Audre Lorde, Barbara Smith, and the Combahee River Collective demanded an intersectional politick among feminists and Leftists. Still, Black trans people were largely absent from their considerations, leaving their mark largely in separate spaces such as Ballroom culture. Figures from this era, including Marsha P. Johnson, Sir Lady Java, Crystal LaBeija, Miss Major, and Zazu Nova, would be unacknowledged for decades.

By the 1990s, the sociopolitical voice of the trans community grew, leading to the emergence of national trans rights formations like GenderPAC and the National Transgender Advocacy Coalition (NTAC). HRC's executive director at the time, Elizabeth Birch, wavered between antagonism and support for trans inclusion in the larger LGBTQ+ movement. Under her tenure, HRC eventually shifted to publicly advocate for trans people—not just for cis gay men and lesbians. Birch also met with trans leaders and promised to fight for a trans-inclusive version of the Employment Non-Discrimination Act (ENDA), federal legislation prohibiting workplace discrimination based on sexual orientation or gender identity and expression.[13] Unfortunately, over the next decade the bill would be trimmed of its trans-inclusive elements by lawmakers, including Rep. Barney Frank (D-MA), and politicos, leading to its failure of passage.

While the LGBTQ+ national nonprofit landscape has been slow to champion trans leadership, the emergence of the movement for Black lives in 2015 and more intersectional coalitions in social justice in the last decade have inspired a constellation of Black trans-led state and local organizations. A much too short list includes Atlanta's Solutions Not Punishments Collaborative, San Francisco's Transgender, Gender-Variant, and Intersex Justice Project (TGIJP), and New Orleans's BreakOUT! These organizations, and countless others, are playing a central role in advocating for equality and liberation. Their advocacy around Black trans dignity, power, and vitality assures me that being Black and trans today is better than when I first began my gender transition more than a decade ago.

Still, much work remains to be done to ensure that transgender people are treated with dignity and respect in the United States—and are fully included in mainstream American democracy. Macro-movements still cling to systems of oppression that invisibilize trans people. Within LGBTQ+ communities, cis people still hold the reins of our nonprofits despite often acknowledging that Black trans people are the most marginalized within our spaces. Those organizations that do not hire and support Black trans people have become obsolete because they often claim to be meaningfully intervening in the discrimination and violence that we face but are unable to truly show evidence for this work. Even when trans people are represented professionally, we often face barriers to equitable treatment and career growth. Nonprofits must address the white supremacy, cissexism, and constrained ideas of respectability that loom over their programming and strategic agendas.

Similarly, Black legacy and emerging organizations must address their own homophobia and transphobia. Many prominent Black-led organizations have yet to make a major concerted effort to fully integrate Black LGBTQ+ people within their ranks. As a whole, Black liberation movements have not prioritized dismantling cisheteropatriarchy—the system of power that privileges those who are male and straight—or the violence it incites. Dialogues about Black cis men being the leading perpetrators of violence against Black women and LGBTQ+ folks ignore the fact that various societal structures have created the conditions for these behaviors. Furthermore, the mainstream feminist movement must address its lingering white supremacy as well as its transexclusionary practices. There must be a concerted effort—on the local, state, and national level—to incorporate a nonbinary political analysis that considers how patriarchy impacts multiple marginalized genders, not only cisgender white women.

Building a more inclusive democracy in the United States requires us to consider the wrongs of past efforts as well. The decades-long laser focus on marriage equality dimmed the flame and promise of other potentially more wide-ranging goals. If the LGBTQ+ nonprofit structure had wholeheartedly championed an expansive version of ENDA, a major dent might have been made in trans unemployment rates and building more affirming and safe workplaces. Then we would have had arable soil in which to plant a true claim for the passage of the Equality Act, a more wide-ranging bill that would ensure protections beyond employment, in housing, education, and public accommodations.[14] Though it is certainly important for those who believe in social justice to still urge for legislation of this type now, especially to combat the growing anti-LGBTQ+ proposed bills in state legislatures across the country, we also must demand support for political education to combat disinformation in media. Citizens and the federal government should urge the passage of legislation that will hold media conglomerates, especially in the social media space, accountable for regulating hate on their platforms.

All publicly funded institutions should be required to educate and train their workers on gender competency, which includes being able to respectfully and humanely assist all people, especially those of marginalized gender and sex experiences. Even further, our educational system should have core curriculum at all levels centered on building and encouraging diversity. Hate is taught, and teaching compassion and understanding is the antidote.

Lawmakers and leaders must also bind the ties between today's major fights. Reproductive justice, voter suppression, health care access, police brutality, hate violence, climate change, and worker rights are all bound by an essential struggle between those who champion bodily autonomy and self-determination and those who want to restrict them. Instead of burrowing so deeply into the spaces between our identities, we must elevate our shared values, especially in messaging, political education, and storytelling. We need political leadership and a social landscape that recognizes the value of Black trans people's lives. We must also address the long-standing white supremacist, cisheteropatriarchal, brutally capitalist nature of American history and the United States's domineering presence in the world. We must consider how we can move from an exploitative and dominating animus into a nation that values true egalitarianism.

I am heartened by the history of Black trans women who have left their mark throughout time and have made it possible for me to be so brazen and bold in my convictions. Without them, I would not be able to move through this world, acknowledging my transness in everyday life with pride. I would not have been able to shift the perspectives of a would-be transphobic cis man to understanding that Black trans people are real and very much deserving of full respect and rights. Thanks to my Black transcestors, I believe there is power and potentiality in Black trans leadership.

Part II

BUILDING POWER

ON POLITICAL REPRESENTATION

Aimee Allison

I am a woman of democratic faith. I was born into it. The powerful stream of this faith stretches back to the earliest days of the country—it is the faith of Black women before me who believed that liberation was possible despite the injustices prevalent here. Black women of the past believed, as do I now, that our fates are bound with others and that peace and justice should be our founding moral code. The democracy founded by the enslaver Thomas Jefferson refused to recognize the humanity of Black and Indigenous people, but successive generations of Black women took actions grounded in a deep and abiding belief that we can create a democracy that fully acknowledges the dignity and humanity of all people.

The heart of American democracy is about promises—that a nation best serves its people when the people rule themselves.

And yet we know that American democracy is a history of broken promises. An inclusive democracy—one that includes all people regardless of their race, gender, sexual orientation, and social status—does not yet exist. Our nation was built on the promise of democracy, but in practice it privileges whiteness above all else. But democratic faith—the complete trust and confidence that an inclusive and multiracial democracy can one day become a reality—guides my path today.

I believe we still have time to make a multiracial democracy the cultural norm—and to create a reality in which Black Americans do not have to fear violence or threats when speaking out or holding public office. We still have time to invest in leaders who reflect the full diversity of the United States. Full political representation—representation that encompasses all the dimensions of our identities, including race, ethnicity, gender, sexual preference, ability, religion, age, and economic status—is necessary to create the kind of democracy I envision.

Black women have been the vanguards for an American democracy not yet realized. Even as we have suffered and sacrificed to bring another, better form of life into being, we have not lost faith that democracy could and should be the engine for this change. We believe in what is possible—even when that very possibility seems outlandish and outrageous to others. We work toward a better future, even if we will never see the results in our lifetimes.

Democratic faith is born of heartbreak. My Black father and white mother started our family only a few years after the Supreme Court's 1967 *Loving* decision, which legalized interracial marriages. It was a hopeful time, an era now called "the Second Reconstruction," when Congress passed social welfare legislation and civil rights laws in an effort to expand the rights of Black Americans.

In 1973 I climbed onto my father's rocking chair with a heavy illustrated book called *Alistair Cooke's America*.[1] I loved the weight of the book. I felt such joy flipping through the colorful, glossy pages. The book, written by a British man, was a story of America. I thought I knew this story. I had been learning about American history in school and reciting the Pledge of Allegiance—"one nation under God." The book was an extravagant telling of this story in images: Midwestern wheat fields waving in the sunlight, the red-golds of the Grand Canyon, and New York City at night.

As I flipped through its pages, the colors turned to gray. I stared at a black and white photograph of a common Depression-era atrocity. Gathered on an Indiana night, a mob of white men and women clustered around the broad base of a large tree. Their faces were either filled with indifference or uplifted in exhilaration. One man with piercing eyes and a toothbrush mustache pointed toward broken figures hanging high in the branches. Two Black boys, their heads bloodied and bowed, their mutilated bodies barely covered in tattered clothing, hung from ropes. They had been lynched by the crowd.[2]

I had only ever seen one image of death before: Jesus on the cross, mounted on the wall of the African Methodist Episcopal Church that my father took me to on Sundays. The lynching photo in Cooke's book left me feeling uneasy. All the people in the photo—*all the people*—looked like members of my own family. The smirking man with the narrow tie and sharp, peg lateral teeth, the pale girls with glossy hair, leaning into each other, and the martyred dead boys with curled hair could have been my forebears.

In that moment, I began to understand the meaning of racial terror. White people publicly tortured and murdered Black people because they refused to accept a democracy that would confer equality on Black Americans. Through the heartbreak, I heard a refrain—*things do not have to be this way*. My family members, Black and white, were bound together in this twisted family tree. That story was my story. It was our nation's story. There comes a moment in a person's life when they must decide what to do when faced with a painful truth, and at that moment, I could have pushed the feeling away, felt shame, or denied that the photo had anything to do with me. Instead, I chose to confront it and made a pledge that I would do everything I could to make real the ideals of American democracy. I decided to answer the call to shape a new country, to commit to making a new world.

The tradition of democratic faith began almost 250 years ago—not with the Declaration of Independence but with Black women like the poet Phillis Wheatley. Born in West Africa, Wheatley became a founding mother of a nation striving to be governed with love, justice, and democracy. "In every human Breast," she wrote in 1774, "God has implanted a Principle, which we call Love of Freedom; it is impatient of Oppression, and pants for Deliverance."[3] Her words capture the essence of maintaining a democratic faith—clinging to what is possible despite the bitter realities of discouragement, pain, and violence. Wheatley's message offers a beacon of hope for the future.

In the United States today, many are trying to derail the work of those who embrace democratic faith. These individuals reject the idea that we must build a multiracial and inclusive democracy to match our multicultural populace. Even now, elected leaders who incited white supremacists to challenge the results of the 2020 presidential election and installed legislative voting barriers still hold office and have not been held accountable for their actions. How can we fortify ourselves in the face of those who are emboldened to enforce the old caste system that undermines full citizenship for all?

Here is where my own democratic faith emerges. Even though there are currently no Black women in the U.S. Senate and there has never been a Black woman governor, I believe both are possible. The structures and current cultural norms that create roadblocks on our path to holding higher office can change. There can be no inclusive multiracial democracy without Black women holding these offices, and I believe it will one day become a reality.

I was in Washington, D.C., with a hundred women leaders on the day the Emmett Till anti-lynching bill was finally passed in 2022—after more than two hundred attempts since 1900.[4] It was the final week of Women's History Month, and Vice President Kamala Harris, who had cosponsored the bill during her time in the U.S. Senate, spoke to us at a backyard gathering at her official residence. The bill acknowledged the horror of 150 years of lynching in the United States. It classified the act as a hate crime and empowered the federal government to prosecute it as such. It was the fulfilment of journalist Ida B. Wells-Barnett's dream. She had dedicated her life to bearing witness to the crimes and calling for change in the United States.[5] When Vice President Harris invoked Wells-Barnett at our gathering that night, I felt my heart break with gratitude for a lifelong dream finally realized.

So many Black women in our past and present share Wells-Barnett's vision to create a more just and equal society. Today, as several states impose voter suppression laws, Black women such as Stacey Abrams demonstrate the democratic possibilities in her home state of Georgia. Through the grassroots organizing of people of color, Abrams inspired a nation eager to reinvigorate democracy. Although she did not win the governor's seat, her efforts serve as a powerful reminder that we can effect change, no matter how small.

Drawing inspiration from the long line of courageous, principled Black women leaders, we can meet the challenges we face today. So it is my work to change the face of American leadership, supporting women of color who will reshape our democracy and make justice the law of the land. I believe that expanding political representation in the United States to include Black women is one way we can accomplish this goal. As the prominent Black radical activist Angela Davis, argues, "You have to act as if it were possible to radically transform the world. And you have to do it all the time."[6]

We can "radically transform" this nation by working to build an inclusive and multiracial democracy. This requires extending our support to Black women in politics—believing that they are electable and have the skills to lead in every sector of society. During my many years dedicated to supporting those who embody the character of democratic faith, I have come to recognize barriers, both visible and invisible, that impede Black women's ability to win seats. I have seen party operatives tell political donors not to back a candidate because they assume the candidate cannot win an election. I have seen the media dismiss Black women candidates as "difficult." And I have seen excellent Black women candidates attempt to run for office without a full staff because they simply do not have the resources. In 2022, Black and brown women were subjected to millions of dollars' worth of attack ads that poisoned the media landscape and discouraged many from voting. These practices must end so we can open up opportunities for Black women to hold leadership roles and to move us closer to an inclusive and multiracial democracy.

There are other steps we can take too. We can change our culture with books, movies, and art that celebrate multiracial democracy and its possibilities for the United States. This might include nationwide programs for children and young adults focused on telling stories of American renewal and calling a new generation into action. We can also invest millions of dollars in on-the-ground organizing led by local groups that build multiracial coalitions and focus on historically underrepresented communities. We must tell the truth about the long history of lynchings and other tactics that attempted to diminish the political power of Black people. We must hold those currently in office accountable for their actions in subverting democracy and advancing the cause of white supremacy.

Black women will have greater political representation—at the local, state, and national levels—if we pass the Equal Rights Amendment, which would advance equality for all women and help to level the playing field for Black women. We should take note of the agenda proposed by the organization Demos, which includes passing universal voter registration to codify the right to vote in the Constitution, and removing unnecessary hurdles to the participation of small donors to democratize the influence of money in our political system.[7]

Four million people are living under the U.S. flag without the right to sovereignty in Puerto Rico, Guam, the U.S. Virgin Islands, American Samoa, the Northern Mariana Islands, and Washington, D.C. As Demos proposes, they need self-determination, which would finally give millions of individuals the right, guaranteed under international human rights law, to "freely determine their political status."[8]

Those who have come before us modeled the way forward: even in the most challenging of times in our nation, they maintained democratic faith. It is my hope that more Americans will realize they were born into a grand faith tradition, stewarded by Black women, a tradition that could help lead us to a better future. Our unfinished business is the possibility of a new nation that includes all of us. Black feminist bell hooks said it best: "Our freedom is sweet. It will be sweeter when we are all free."[9]

ON RACIAL INEQUITIES IN HEALTH CARE

Dr. Rhea Boyd

In a wealthy democracy, survival should be a given. Any nation that has the resources and the political organization to create and sustain equality should also offer equal rights, protections, and access to vital resources to its residents. Survival—an outcome derived from those shared benefits—should be all but assumed. Yet if you measure the success of a democracy by the number of people who can survive in it, a deep failing of American democracy is that fewer and fewer Americans can, particularly in recent years.

Despite spending more money on health care than any other country in the world, the United States has a troublingly low life expectancy.[1] In other nations, marginal increases in health care spending result in marginal increases in life expectancy. But Americans, just by virtue of being born and living in the United

States, can expect to die at a younger age than their peers in Germany, Japan, Chile, and Cuba.[2] Even in recent years, while other wealthy nations' mortality rates have rebounded from the ongoing scourge of COVID-19, American life expectancy continues to fall to devastating new lows. According to the Centers for Disease Control and Prevention (CDC), the successive drops in life expectancy in 2020 and 2021 represent the largest two-year decline in life expectancy in the United States since the early 1920s.[3]

The ever-shrinking American life span exposes a rot at the core of American democracy. Everyone can be disappeared here. Men. Women. Children. The elderly. The immunocompromised. Those who have chronic underlying conditions. Those who are healthy but at the wrong place at the wrong time. Those whose gender defies the binary. Those whose behavior defies norms. Those whom police wantonly target. Those whom society predominantly ignores. Those who venture into a church or a school or a grocery store. Those who are isolated. Those who are beloved. The oppressed. The repressed. The impoverished. The rich. The victims of a predatory political economy.

In America, there is no presumption of survival. And now the disappearing has become a way to govern.

In 2017, Yale historian Timothy Snyder coined the term *sadopopulism* to characterize how oligarchs safeguard their power.[4] As he describes it, sadopopulism is a way of governing through pain. By issuing policies that hurt Americans, such as regressive tax breaks for the rich and cuts in health care benefits for the indigent, this approach generates material loss, anxiety, and fear. Racialized others are made to bear the brunt of these losses and are blamed for them. Rather than offering Americans a vision of the future in which everyone can thrive, sadopopulism resurrects racist grievances from the past. It redirects the target of Americans' ire from harmful policies and policy makers onto racialized others. Sadopopulism then thrives on the rot. Everyone *will be* harmed, but the harm will be unevenly distributed. People will be disappeared from society, and some will die. But as long as those racialized as "them" are disappeared and are dying more than "us," sadopopulists expect Americans to accept it. And in 2016, too many did.

Prior to the 2016 presidential election, life in the United States was predicated on deep inequalities reinforced by centuries of policies that kept people tired, sick, or both. Health inequities, or the preventable and unjust disparities in outcomes between "us" and "them," therefore, were often understood as the fruition of centuries of predation.[5]

Post-2016, those same inequalities persist, but they must also be understood as the promise and appeal of an emerging type of governance. Health inequities are not simply inadvertent by-products of the unsettling and recent turn in American politics toward sadopopulism. They are the platform. Elected officials from presidential hopefuls to school board candidates are now boldly undermining America's democratic processes and protections to offer up policies that will hurt people en masse—with the caveat that racialized others will face the greatest losses. And too many Americans are accepting it.

Just look at the COVID-19 era. It has been full of these kinds of morbid acceptances. Those who refuse to adhere to basic public health precautions such as wearing face masks or maintaining their vaccinations have accepted that the elderly and immunocompromised will disproportionately fill our hospitals and that some will never return home. The social media plutocrats who failed to shield their users from intentional distortions and disinformation have accepted the groundswell of anti-vax propaganda that unleashed polio in New York and measles in Ohio, leaving the children who are too young for vaccination disproportionately vulnerable to preventable disease.[6] And the elected officials who chose not to push for additional funding for public health interventions now tacitly accept that the disproportionate toll of COVID-19 will continue to fall on those who have fewer resources to weather the perpetual storm.

Too many Americans accept that the prosperity and longevity promised to them are pieced together from the truncated futures of others—especially Indigenous and Black people. Even now, as Americans die prematurely at unprecedented rates, Indigenous and Black Americans have the shortest life spans of any humans born and living in the wealthy world.[7] As University of Chicago historian Thomas Holt writes, "Could it be that in such a marketplace, black bodies—no longer a means of production—have become a means of consumption?"[8] Could it be that in the democratic nation that spends more on health care than any other, the collective investment in abiding racist divides still trumps the possibility of a shared future?

The short answer is yes.

But there is another way. There is a type of governance where longevity is a function not of shared pain but of shared benefits. It is a multiracial and inclusive democracy.

Generations of Americans have believed that a multiracial and inclusive democracy could exist here. It has been a core tenet of liberation and labor movements alike. And while some treat it as more aspirational than achievable, the beginnings already exist.

Consider Medicaid, the means-tested federal and state health insurance program. The program covers close to one in five Americans, just about half of all births and—when combined with the Children's Health Insurance Program, a government-funded health insurance program for children whose income is too high for Medicaid—46 percent of all children. It also covers over 10 million American adults and children with disabilities. During the federal public health emergency to address COVID-19, access to the program ballooned to more than 90 million Americans, a historic increase in its coverage.[9] If Medicaid's ability to deepen multiracial democracy is judged solely by participation, then as the single largest health insurer in the nation that also disproportionately covers Black, Hispanic, and Indigenous people, it is remarkably effective. And if the rot at the core of American democracy is, at least in part, the nation's inability to foster longevity despite its enormous resources, Medicaid may be a critical demonstration of what it will take to fortify democracy against its newest assailants.

A 2021 analysis found that states that expanded Medicaid under the Affordable Care Act had lower all-cause mortality rates than states that did not. Notably, reductions in all-cause mortality were greatest within expansion states that had higher proportions of women and non-Hispanic Black residents.[10] These findings suggest that access to Medicaid can safeguard Americans from premature death and that women and non-Hispanic Black residents may benefit the most from its expansion. In short, Medicaid helps people survive here, particularly those often rendered vulnerable. Participation in Medicaid also has been associated with decreased mortality rates for the elderly, social mobility for children across racial groups, and higher cumulative wages for women in early adulthood.[11]

The expansion of Medicaid should be a cornerstone of efforts to advance multiracial democracy, given its impact on mortality rates; its broad inclusion of Americans made most vulnerable by the nation's predatory political economy; and its disproportionate benefit for those historically excluded from full participation in American democracy. And while some favor Medicare—a government-funded health insurance program for Americans over age sixty-five—as the blueprint for universal health care in America, a strong case can be made that Medicaid is the ideal place to start. In the face of sadopopulism, rugged individualism, and the ravages of capitalism, Medicaid is a critical battleground to achieve and experience a participatory America, where those who are made most vulnerable are most protected through collective investment and benefit.

With Medicaid as the foundation of what is possible here, perhaps Americans could expect more from their health care experience. What could it look like, for example, to broaden Americans' conception of health care beyond what government-funded health insurance traditionally covers? Traditional services like medical, vision, and dental care are important and serve a valuable role in the care experience, but they need not be the totality of it.

Care could include medical, dental, and vision but also mental health care, home health care, childcare, elder care, companionship care for the lonely, and grief care for the bereaved. It could include income subsidies to support food as medicine, housing as an intervention, clean air as a prophylactic, mobility aids and accessibility infrastructure for the disabled, and rest, recreation, and paid leave as protected resources that enable families to care for their members and their communities.

Like Medicaid, care could be free (paid for by tax dollars so that every American would have access to it) and universal (available to all Americans regardless of their age, income level, or disability status). Rather than enrolling as individuals, as is common within the insurance marketplace, in a reimagined government-funded marketplace, people could enroll as a family, which could be delineated by blood relation or personal selection. This arrangement would allow people to be considered as members of collective units who care for each other. Such an approach nurtures the relationships that form the core of a functioning democracy—neighbors, families, and friends.

The goals of care could be centered on healing family divisions, restoring loving connections within community, maintaining the autonomy of those with special needs, compassionately supporting people's mental well-being, creating financial security and housing stability for families, expanding accommodations for those with disabilities, and serving the infrastructural needs of neighborhoods. These goals could surpass survival and begin to approximate a society that is thriving. Within this type of participatory society, health would not simply be a measure of an individual's ability to withstand harm. Rather, health would be an accounting of the distribution of opportunities, the breadth of viable shelter, the quality of the water, the breathability of the air, the richness of the food supply, and the ability of public infrastructure to maintain conditions that support the workforce, guard against disaster, and respond to crises. Health would become an estimation of a thriving, multiracial democracy.

This future is not far off, and most Americans are already invested in it. The U.S. health care system is currently a $4 trillion industry. The health care sector alone accounts for nearly one-fifth of our nation's gross domestic product.[12] And a 2022 Pew Research poll found that reducing health care costs is the second-highest national priority for Americans.[13]Americans already want, and pay an extraordinary amount for, care that is only a fraction of what is possible.

And yet paradoxically, a disturbing willingness to accept mass death remains in the United States. The health inequities that emerge from such acceptance—measured in time lost, futures stolen, lives foreshortened, and relationships severed by the certitude of death—are evidence of the dogged persistence of inequality and emerging threats to democracy here. As in any society built upon the forced suffering of some, everyone in the United States is at risk of experiencing harm.

Too many do not survive chronic illness. Too many birthing

people do not survive childbirth. Too many babies do not survive their first year. Too many adults do not survive addiction. Too many children do not survive school. Too many Americans do not survive isolation, immiseration, discrimination, violence, and disease.

Disappearance and death have become the rule rather than an exception. This is the rot that exists in American democracy. Using Medicaid as a lever to advance multiracial and inclusive democracy here is a step toward survival and the future.

ON COALITION BUILDING

Donna Brazile

Throughout U.S. history, the struggle by Black Americans for equality and equity has required coalition building. As an oppressed minority, we have never had the numerical strength or the wealth and power to transform our country for the better all by ourselves. Generations of Black people have understood the value of building multiracial coalitions based on the goals that unite us and our shared commitment to justice.

Without the support of people from other races, Black people alone could not have ended slavery in the United States or brought an end to the legally enforced racism that followed. We continue to rely on multiracial coalitions today to fuel our ongoing efforts to end voter suppression, job and housing discrimination, and other manifestations of racism. In addition, Black candidates need votes from people of other races to win elections outside Black-majority areas. Half of the record-high sixty Black people elected to Congress in 2022 represent congressional districts or states where the plurality of the population is white.[1] Without coalitions with our allies, Black Americans would be far worse off today, and fewer of us would hold elected office.

As a child growing up near New Orleans during the 1960s in the dying days of Jim Crow, I was never taught by my parents to hate white people or anyone else. Over the course of my career, I have been blessed to have worked with many white, Latino, and Asian Americans who were just as committed as I am to opening the American dream to everyone. These allies worked hard—sometimes putting their personal safety at great risk—to achieve our shared goals.

The multiracial coalitions that Black people have successfully built have dedicated themselves to making the United States live up to the stirring words of the Declaration of Independence: "That all men are created equal, that they are endowed by their Creator with certain unalienable rights, that among these are life, liberty and the pursuit of happiness."[2] *All* should mean exactly that: every human being, regardless of race, gender, religion, sexual orientation, or gender identity. Unfortunately, the primary author of the Declaration—future president Thomas Jefferson—enslaved over six hundred Black Americans over the course of his lifetime.[3] Moreover, most of the signers of the Declaration in 1776 enslaved Black people, at a time when slavery was legal in all thirteen British colonies. And almost half the delegates to the Constitutional Convention in 1787 enslaved Black people, as did at least twelve U.S. presidents at some point in their lives, including eight while they were in office.[4]

Talk about hypocrisy! In reality, for much of U.S. history, the words *all men* in the Declaration applied only to white men. Black people and women of all races were denied many rights, including the right to vote, long after the United States became an independent nation. Systemic racism and sexism remain deeply ingrained in American society—despite absurd denials by many Republican elected officials today—and our efforts to eliminate these forms of discrimination continue.

In the brief and superficial treatment that most U.S. schools give to the role of Black people in American history, most of the attention goes to slavery, the Civil War, the civil rights movement, and the achievements of a few outstanding Black men. Abolitionist Frederick Douglass, scientist and inventor Dr. George Washington Carver (both born into slavery), civil rights leader the Rev. Dr. Martin Luther King, Jr., civil rights champion and unsuccessful presidential candidate the Rev. Jesse Jackson, and President Barack Obama are among the small number of Black men whose stories are centered in textbooks. They have certainly earned it.

However, 50 percent of Black people are women, and the critically important role they have played in building the coalitions and leading the campaigns so essential to Black advancement has often gone unrecognized. This omission reflects the marginalization of Black history in U.S. schools. It is also a consequence of the way the accomplishments of women of all races have been largely ignored in societies around the world. In the fight to end slavery, Jim Crow, and other forms of racism, Black women have been among the hardest and most committed workers. But these sisters have usually been relegated to supporting roles, as Black men took the spotlight in leadership roles—and received most of the credit.

I experienced this sexism when I began working in civil rights and Democratic political campaigns in the 1970s and '80s. Male colleagues often saw stuffing envelopes, taking notes at meetings, typing, making photocopies, brewing coffee, picking up food, making travel arrangements, and cleaning as "women's work." As a Black woman, I had to fight to get a seat at the table where decisions were being made. Rep. Shirley Chisholm (D-NY), who in 1968 became the first Black woman elected to Congress, had similar experiences. In 1972 she became the first Black person and only the second woman (following white Republican senator Margaret Chase Smith of Maine in 1964) to seek a major party presidential nomination—and many Americans viewed her candidacy as hopeless. The idea of a Black man becoming president of the United States seemed impossible to many Americans in 1972, and the idea of a Black woman becoming president seemed even more of a fantasy.[5]

Since Chisholm's presidential run, Black women—who are primarily Democrats—have made significant progress in politics and government. In 2023, twenty-eight of the 435 members of the House of Representatives are Black women—about 6 percent. However, there are no Black women in the hundred-member U.S. Senate, following the 2021 resignation of Democratic senator Kamala Harris of California—to become the first Black and first Asian American vice president. Harris is one of only two Black women to serve in the Senate in U.S. history.[6] No Black woman has ever been elected governor of a state, and no woman has ever been president of the United States.[7]

In 2023, Black women hold ten statewide elected offices, along with 368 seats in state legislatures (5 percent of all seats). In addition, Black women served as mayors of nine of the hundred largest U.S. cities in 2023, including Chicago, Los Angeles, San Francisco, St. Louis, New Orleans, and Washington, D.C.[8] In 2022 Ketanji Brown Jackson became the first Black woman to join the Supreme Court after she was nominated by President Joe Biden and confirmed by the Senate. During his first two years as president, Biden nominated and won Senate confirmation for eleven Black women to serve as federal appeals court judges—more than all former U.S. presidents combined.[9]

African American women today stand on the shoulders of our Black sisters who fought past battles for equality, and we continue their unfinished work. Forming diverse coalitions is a significant part of this history—and it is necessary today as we work toward building an inclusive and multiracial democracy. Where do we go from here to make our country live up to the ideals of the Declaration of Independence? We must work together, despite our ideological differences, to advance policies that would benefit all Americans. That means focusing on our common values—our commitment to strengthening American democracy and ensuring that every citizen has the resources they need to thrive. Our most urgent priorities need to be reversing the setbacks our democracy suffered as a result of the actions of defeated Republican president Donald Trump and the decisions of the far-right Supreme Court. This will require several actions in partnership with diverse coalitions: both Republicans and Democrats need to work together to restore integrity to the electoral process.

First, we can restore faith in elections by demanding that Trump and his supporters who tried to overturn his 2020 reelection loss be held legally accountable. No one—not even a former U.S. president—is above the law. We should also demand that Congress and state governments put mechanisms in place to prevent anyone from stealing a future election and transforming the United States from a democracy into an autocracy. I have worked for Democratic candidates who lost elections—most notably as campaign manager for Vice President Al Gore in his unsuccessful presidential campaign in 2000. Gore did not try to overturn a Supreme Court decision declaring Republican George W. Bush the winner in a very tight race. And he certainly did not mount an elaborate effort—including a deadly riot in the Capitol—to stop Bush from becoming president.

Second, we should demand that Congress and the states restore voting rights eroded by Supreme Court decisions and by Republican states that have enacted laws making it harder for citizens to cast lawful ballots. Lawmakers should make voting quick and easy for every eligible citizen by absentee ballot and in person on Election Day and at least thirty days before. This requires Congress to revive efforts to pass the John R. Lewis Voting Rights Advancement Act, which would modernize and strengthen the Voting Rights Act of 1965.[10] The Social Security cards that almost every adult possesses should be upgraded with photos (at the government's expense) and serve as voter ID cards in states that require such identification. Election Day should also be made a federal holiday to make it easier for people to get to the polls. Seventeen-year-olds should be allowed to preregister to vote so they can cast ballots after turning eighteen. And citizens should be allowed to register to vote when they show up at polling places as late as Election Day. College students should be allowed to vote on their campuses, rather than having to travel to their parents' homes. States and localities should be barred from purging people from voter rolls within ninety days of elections. And nonprofit groups should be allowed to conduct voter education and registration drives. These efforts would significantly expand voter participation in the United States—and it would strengthen our democracy. All Americans, regardless of their political affiliation, will benefit when we expand voter access.

Third, we must call on Congress to restore the freedom of American women to control our own bodies, which was taken away by the 2022 Supreme Court ruling that overturned the right to have an abortion. A federal law barring states from restricting abortion rights before fetal viability is urgently needed.

Fourth, we must pass the George Floyd Justice in Policing Act, which is designed to crack down on police misconduct.[11] Republicans blocked passage of the legislation during the 117th Congress by demanding that it be watered down, even as growing numbers of unarmed Black people are killed by police.

Fifth, we should demand that Congress build on the Affordable Care Act (often referred to as Obamacare) to give all Americans access to affordable health care. This is quite literally a matter of life and death as Republicans have worked to repeal or weaken the Affordable Care Act.

Sixth, we should work to make high-quality affordable education available to everyone in our country, regardless of family income. This investment in our future will pay tremendous dividends. It would create a well-paid educated workforce that will make the United States economically competitive with nations around the world, reduce spending on public assistance, and increase tax revenue. (The more people earn, the more they pay in taxes.) This objective requires increasing federal, state and local funding for public schools, targeted to eliminate the huge gap in per-pupil spending between schools in wealthy suburban communities and low-income communities, where Black people are disproportionately concentrated. It also requires a dramatic increase in funding for college scholarships and low-interest or interest-free loans to help students afford the skyrocketing costs of higher education. Because Black families on average earn less than white families, Black students would particularly benefit.

These six proposals do not represent the totality of the changes we need to make in this nation. However, they should be priorities. To make this vision of a more just and equitable America a reality, the most effective strategy is to build diverse coalitions to help elect progressive candidates at the local, state, and federal levels who will champion these causes. We need to vote, march, volunteer to work on campaigns, donate money to candidates when we can (even if only in small amounts), and urge friends, family members, and colleagues to get involved in the political process. We would make significant strides as a nation if we focused on the common goal of building an inclusive and multiracial democracy that improves the quality of life and expands resources for Americans of all backgrounds. This process is not easy—I know from experience that it is often difficult to build coalitions with those who hold differing views. However, when we make the effort, the results can be rewarding. My time as a member of the National Council on Election Integrity, a bipartisan group of political and civic leaders, reaffirmed my commitment to building coalitions. I worked closely with progressives as well as conservatives such as former Republican National Committee chair Michael Steele. Our mutual commitment to defending the legitimacy of fair elections in the United States bridged ideological divides.

We have plenty of role models—including heroic barrier-breaking Black women such as Shirley Chisholm, Rosa Parks, and Fannie Lou Hamer—to show us how to make this nation a more inclusive democracy. These women worked to address a number of social ills, including segregation, voter suppression, inequities in health care, and economic inequality. And they did so through various strategies, including forging alliances with Americans of diverse backgrounds. Their efforts underscore the power of coalition building as a vital component of any democracy. As we look ahead, we must be committed to working with freedom fighters of diverse racial backgrounds to make necessary changes in American society.

While systemic racism continues to place roadblocks in front of Black Americans—and systemic sexism further impedes the advancement of Black women—the opportunities available to us today are far greater than those that were available to our ancestors. This is good news not just for Black people but for all Americans. Working to build coalitions with our fellow Americans of all backgrounds, struggling against the odds, and convincing people of all races that ending discrimination is in our mutual self-interest is the best way to ensure better days ahead for our nation—and for generations yet unborn.

ON EQUAL PAY FOR BLACK WOMEN

Glynda C. Carr

Black women in the United States dream of the day when we can earn a salary that is equal to that of our white male counterparts. We dream of a day when the concept of equal pay is more than a mere fairy tale. Until then, the reality is that Black women in this country must work almost ten additional months a year—214 days, to be exact—to catch up to white men.[1] We are ready for this story to be over. It is time for a new narrative for Black workers.

During the era of slavery, Black Americans were viewed as property and subjected to a system of domination and exploitation. During the nineteenth and twentieth centuries, Black people attempted to prove their loyalty and patriotism by serving in the U.S. military. During the Civil War and World Wars I and II, for example, they toiled as soldiers, ship caulkers, seamstresses, factory workers, agricultural workers, and railroaders.[2] For some jobs, they were paid only tips. In others, they faced unusual hazards. During the early twentieth century, while the pay was low for Black workers—and the stakes were high—Black Americans were allowed to join the workforce alongside white Americans, even if not for the same wages. White workers were not pleased with this inclusion as the nation suffered the financial scourge of the wars and the Great Depression. So they rallied to lower the wages of Black workers further and even advocated for replacing Black workers with white workers.[3]

The American workplace began to change during the 1930s with President Franklin D. Roosevelt's New Deal. The 1935 Social Security Act, the National Labor Relations Act, and the Fair Labor Standards Act worked in tandem to address race and gender inequity in the U.S. labor force. However, these government reform programs excluded domestic and agricultural workers—overwhelmingly Black women—from receiving benefits.[4]

Given these realities, it is not coincidental that during the modern civil rights movement, Black women emerged as the most vocal champions for pay equity and fairness. Fannie Lou Hamer was one of these outspoken activists. Her childhood experiences—growing up in a sharecropping family in Mississippi—drove her passion to fight for both Black political power and economic justice. As historian Keisha N. Blain points out, Hamer "understood that Black political rights could not be divorced from economic rights and recognized that economic security was fundamental to the struggle for civil rights."[5]

Many Black women championed economic justice during the 1960s and '70s. Shirley Chisholm, the first Black woman elected to Congress and the first woman and African American to run for the presidential nomination of a major political party, was a strong proponent of equal pay for Black women. She often spoke about women's rights as human rights and was a backer of the Equal Rights Amendment (ERA), which would guarantee legal rights to all citizens regardless of sex.

In the House of Representatives on August 10, 1970, Chisholm—before an audience of mostly white men—enthusiastically supported the resolution. The ERA, she argued, "represents one of the most clear-cut opportunities we are likely to have to declare our faith in the principles that shaped our Constitution. It provides a legal basis for attack on the most subtle, most pervasive and most institutionalized form of prejudice that exists. Discrimination against women, solely on the basis of their sex, is so widespread that it seems to many persons normal, natural and right."[6] Her words still ring true today.

The gender gap, used as a systemic tool to push Black women to the bottom of the economic ladder, remains yet another obstacle that we must overcome in order to reach positions of power in the United States. But let's be clear: the pay gap includes all Black women in this country, including those who punch in as hourly trade workers and those working in C-suite leadership positions. This occupational segregation was created by design.

In 2020 the Center for American Progress found that white working women earn eighty-two cents for every dollar earned by white men, while Black women earned sixty-three cents for every dollar earned by white men. Over a Black woman's working life of forty years, she incurs an estimated loss of $964,400.[7] A 2021 report from the Congressional Caucus on Black Women and Girls reaffirmed this grim financial disparity, describing the pay gap between Black women and white men as "America's widest, most pernicious pay gap." The caucus argued that this disparity "is symptomatic of centuries of economic abuse and exploitation designed to relegate a population to the margins of the world's most lucrative economy."[8] Today, as Black women, we shoulder both sexism and racism. While we climb the career ladder, bump our heads on the glass ceiling, and try to play catch-up, we are literally paying the price.

Whether we refer to it as an "unjust practice," "ethnic bias," "racial disparity," or "implicit bias," the pay gap between Black women and white men must be eliminated if we are committed to building an inclusive democracy. The time to make these changes is now. With each passing year, the pay gap continues to widen. The COVID-19 pandemic, which began in 2020, further exacerbated the widening pay gap between Black women and their white male counterparts.[9] Black women also experienced more job loss during the pandemic than other racial groups.[10] These women were pushed out of the workforce in some cases because of the lack of access to childcare. Between February 2020 and March 2021, American women lost more than 4.6 million jobs, according to the National Women's Law Center.[11] Now more than ever, we need to respond. It's time for those with the political and financial power in the United States to join forces to come up with strategies to resolve this issue.

When I co-founded Higher Heights in 2011, lower pay was one of the issues I was determined to address. As an organization, Higher Heights educates, supports, and rallies for Black women, and works to elect Black women who will fight for progressive legislation that will best reflect the most pressing intersectional issues we face daily.[12]

Over the years, I have worked closely with policy makers across the country to devise strategies for closing the wage gap between Black women and white men. One of the organization's goals during these early years was to expand Black women's leadership opportunities to ensure that we have more policy makers who have a deep and intimate understanding of the devastating consequences of the pay gap between Black women and white men.

Since 2011, the organization played an instrumental role in electing eleven Black women to Congress, and we increased the number of Black women holding statewide executive office, including the first Black woman to serve as New York State attorney general. We also supported Vice President Kamala Harris during her run for Senate and her bid for the presidency. We helped to advocate for then–Vice President Joe Biden to select a Black woman to be his running mate. As a result of these efforts, we now have a Black woman serving as vice president who understands the urgency of addressing the wage gap for Black women in the United States.

On the heels of summer, around August or September, the nation observes Black Women's Equal Pay Day. It's the approximate day on the calendar when a working Black woman would have caught up to the previous year's annual earnings of a white man.[13] The observance, which began in 1996, marks an existing inequity that we are reminded of every day when we go to work. What if Black women were actually paid what we are owed? What if we were treated as equals in the workplace?

All Americans must do their part to ensure that we are making strides toward equity and justice for Black women in the workforce. This is a fundamental step toward building a just and inclusive democracy. Black women should not be paid less for the same labor as their white male counterparts simply on account of our sex and race.

The current wage gap in the United States is an affront to democracy. If we are determined to create an equal playing field for all Americans, we cannot look the other way.

Eliminating the current pay disparity has broad implications for the future of American democracy. According to the National Partnership for Women and Families, if the sex—and race—wage gap were eliminated today, Black women in the United States would be able to afford two years of childcare, 130 more weeks of food for their families, and nineteen more months of rent.[14]

And this is just the beginning. Eliminating the wage gap means that Black women in the United States would have the ability to pay off their student loans. They would not have to work overtime or hold more than one job simply to make ends meet. They would be able to spend more time with family and practice self-care—steps that certainly would enhance their overall quality of life.

It truly would not take much action to close the gap. The answer lies in making immediate changes to hiring practices, promotion policies, salary transparency, and benefits packages for all employees. It also requires the passage of the Paycheck Fairness Act, which would prevent employers from paying employees lower wages on the basis of their race, gender, or other social category. Further, the bill would strengthen the Equal Pay Act of 1963 so women can challenge wage discrimination, and it would amend the Civil Rights Act of 1964 to require the Equal Employment Opportunity Commission to collect sex, race, and national origin data from employers for potential enforcement. Under this act, employees—including Black women—would be protected from job retaliation and wage secrecy.[15] As of this writing, while the House has passed the Paycheck Fairness Act, the Senate has not, calling it an opening to increase litigation against employers and burden small businesses, government agencies, and corporations.[16] Keep in mind there are zero Black women in the U.S. Senate—a missing and much-needed voice in this debate.

Though this will not happen overnight, these initiatives alone could help to close the wage gap in the United States. And we need federal accountability to make sure they all take place.

In August 2021, Rep. Alma Adams's (D-NC) office reported that for a Black woman working full time, year round, in the United States, the median annual pay was $41,098. That means that Black women earned $24,110 less than their average white, non-Hispanic male counterparts. Adams's office concluded that if this trend continues, Black women will have to wait one hundred years before true wage equality becomes a reality.[17] We refuse to wait one hundred years to be paid equally. And we are tired of simply imagining a better day.

Pay equity is a necessary part of a democratic society. Women continue to realize the importance of pay equity legislation, which is now being introduced in states around the country. Pay discrepancy undermines democracy. It hurts American families, especially during the most difficult times. We cannot ignore this issue—unequal pay will only continue to grow if it remains unchecked. Black women, like all other women, deserve to be paid fairly and not a cent less. As Vice President Kamala Harris argued at the White House Equal Pay Day Fairness Summit in 2022, "To build an economy that works for all of us, we must build an economy that works for women. . . . An economy that works for women works for everyone."[18]

I would add that to build an inclusive democracy that meets the needs of all Americans, we must eliminate the current wage gap. There is too much at stake. Advancing equal pay for Black women would not only improve the lives of Black women, it would make us all stronger as a nation. It's time to close the gap in what Black women are paid merely because they are women and Black. Our democracy depends on it.

ON POLITICAL POWER

Alicia Garza

The so-called racial reckoning of 2020 is woefully incomplete. The diversity and social justice councils have all but shuttered their doors. The commitments from corporations to hire differently, spend differently, and be different have all but dissipated, their commitments unfulfilled.

A backlash to Black power has since ensued, with forceful attempts to push back against the cultural, economic, and political changes that a racial reckoning in this country would undoubtedly usher in. Familiar outrage about "crime and violence" has reverberated across the nation, an attempt to weaken and neutralize the support of white Americans for racial justice. Meanwhile, a familiar accusation of corruption and "freeloading" has targeted Black people and other people of color to limit their support and participation in racial justice movements.

In the meantime, an extreme faction of the conservative movement in America—and across the globe—has not wavered in its attempts to contend for power, influence, and authority. More than thirty years of steadfast organizing and advocacy have resulted in political power that has eliminated fundamental rights, changed the balance of power on the U.S. Supreme Court for at least a generation, and begun to normalize political violence and terror to stifle dissent.

The question of "where do we go from here?" has never been more profound—not even when it was asked by the Rev. Dr. Martin Luther King, Jr., in 1967.

For King, the winning combination for self-actualization and self-determination was cultural confidence, economic power, and political power. Black men fully embracing their manhood, coupled with gaining buying and spending power and the ability to make the powerful capitulate to racial justice demands, was the recipe for justice and equality.[1] In today's society, what is the winning combination for the self-actualization and self-determination of Black people?

While I agree with King in many respects, some important components are missing from his formulation of what is needed for freedom and justice for all Black people. The key to freedom is political power. And this is an imperative for democracy.

To best understand political power, we have to understand power as a framework. Power is the ability to make the rules and change the rules. There are different forms of power, but ultimately, power is about the ability to change the laws, make the laws, change the culture, and redefine the culture according to one's agenda.

I define political power as the ability to determine who represents you and what agenda they advance on your behalf. Political power is the ability to decide where resources go and don't go and why. If politics is the science and art of who gets what resources and when and why they receive these resources, then political power is the *ability to determine* who gets what, when, and why.

I include culture as a part of my framework around power because our lives are not just shaped by laws, policies, and edicts. We are also governed by the common sense of the culture that surrounds us. Social theorist Antonio Gramsci called this common sense "hegemony"—the cultural norms surrounding what we understand as right and wrong, good and bad, acceptable and not acceptable.[2]

Ai-jen Poo, president of the National Domestic Workers Alliance and a longtime organizer and movement builder, developed a framework for thinking about the types of power that movements need to build at any given moment to achieve the freedom and justice that would correct the oppression and injustice that so many face today. According to Poo, there are at least five forms of power that we must build—political power, narrative power, disruptive power, economic power, and modeling power.

These five forms of power tie culture and policy together. Narrative power is the ability to control the story of who we are and who we can be, together. Disruptive power is the ability to intervene when injustice is happening—think direct action. Economic power is the ability to shape how we produce, consume, and distribute goods and services. Modeling power is our ability to popularize alternatives to the status quo.[3]

Political power, then, is the ability to determine who represents you and to make your agenda the one that sets the terms for everyone.

Cultural and policy changes must go hand in hand to create a new set of conditions that will allow Black communities to thrive. Like Dr. King, many who seek Black power, freedom, and justice tend to focus on some forms of power and not on others.

At the same time, we often confuse power with empowerment, which by necessity stops short of power that can transform our material conditions.

When Dr. King asked, "Where do we go from here?," he declared proudly that Black people had begun to adopt and embrace their "manhood," by which he likely meant empowerment, a sense of self-esteem and cultural pride resulting from the demand that we not only be afforded respect but also that we respect ourselves enough to fight for ourselves and our basic dignity.[4] That King saw this level of respect and empowerment as the realm of men alludes to the masculinist vision of many Black leaders. Too often freedom, justice, and power are considered the purview of men.

Having cultural power—a sense of pride and respect by those who have been marginalized or disenfranchised in some way—can never be enough to achieve the changes we seek for ourselves or the broader society. The last decade of #BlackLivesMatter has shown us that cultural power is insufficient on its own to change the laws that legitimize racial injustice.

During the so-called racial reckoning of 2020, corporations could not get enough of the symbolism of Black lives mattering. We saw more Black commentators and anchors on primetime news shows. One day while I was in search of mindless reality television shows, a Black Lives Matter channel appeared on my television. Nancy Pelosi, who was then Speaker of the House of Representatives, kneeled in a staged photo with Senate majority leader Chuck Schumer, flanked by prominent members of the Congressional Black Caucus, draped in kente cloth.[5] Black Lives Matter signs, gear, and flags proliferated, finding themselves in windows of suburban white communities.

Today, only a few years later, the C-suites in major corporations remain predominantly white. Black commentators and anchors on primetime television have dwindled if not disappeared. Police reform never made it past the finish line, even after a Black man named George Floyd was choked to death under the knee of a white Minneapolis Police Department officer on camera for the world to watch. The signs in the windows have faded, and I can't seem to find that channel anymore on my television. An economic system that benefits from racial injustice adapts to absorb Black cultural pride, allowing it to be bought and sold—and to disappear just as easily.

It's not uncommon for some to try and build cultural power based on a thinly veiled disdain for poor and working-class Black people. Black empowerment often becomes a way to further the us-versus-them dynamic, carving out access for freedom and justice to those with the means to access it. As such, Black empowerment becomes an exclusive club rather than a tool with which to obtain dignity and respect for all.

Empowerment—feeling good about ourselves within our current circumstances—and cultural pride do not equate to being able to make and change the rules so that self-esteem is a result of policies that govern our lives and disseminate resources equitably. Too many confuse empowerment with power, and as a result, we shortchange the scope of the radical transformations that are possible.

Today too many align themselves with Dr. King's message of cultural power at the expense—and even at times in the absence—of a rigorous examination of his call for political power. Even he glossed over political power in his directions to the Southern Christian Leadership Conference, when he attempted to answer the question of where we go from here.

To build an effective and inclusive democracy where the freedom of all Americans is protected and upheld, we must be concerned with the question of building political power. This means building Black political power that is independent of the existing political parties, Republican and Democrat, and instead is concerned with how political parties are utilized as tools.

To get there, we must address at least three core strategies: restoring the responsibility of government to communities in partnership with elected officials; engaging communities regularly, democratically, and substantively in the decisions that impact their lives; and ensuring that when the people you elect to represent you act against your interests, there are consequences.

One evening I sat on the porch with a dear friend who has played an instrumental role in working to save our democracy. She and I discussed an upcoming election cycle, lamenting the ongoing challenge we faced from candidates who did not consider themselves to be accountable to Black communities—a challenge stemming from a lack of political power.

My friend emphasized the need to also hold corporations accountable for the havoc they wreak on our communities, even to the point of our extracting concessions and resources from them through tactics like boycotts. While I agreed with all she said, I added that the overall challenge facing our democracy is to focus on extracting concessions from private entities who are by their design unaccountable to communities. CEOs are not democratically elected by their customers, and their responsibility is only to the economic solvency of the company itself.

By contrast, the government is accountable to communities by design. Despite its many flaws, the whole premise of democracy is that it is for the people, by the people. While we can, should, and must hold corporations accountable, our government must be doing the same, and in fact, the government should be taking the lead. Policy must regulate and construct the role that corporations play in our society, in our economy, and in our democracy. Policy is determined by legislators who we elect to represent us and our interests. Legislators who take the interests of their constituents to state legislatures and city halls to design policy are a product of effective political power.

Corporations have figured out how to build political power—they buy it. Democracy is under dire threat due to the role that money plays in politics. Rather than campaigning to represent the interests of all Americans, most elected officials spend the vast majority of their time trying to raise money to be able to keep their elected position. Ask any elected official in the country, and they will detail a sordid web of decisions they are forced to make every day to satisfy their donors—many of whom are corporations and industry giants.

If you've ever wondered why we can't stop mass shootings or crime in our communities; why we can't interrupt the devastating impact of climate catastrophe due to unchecked climate change; why millions of Americans remain uninsured and without health care; why the population of people without homes and without food continues to balloon, it is, in part, because our elected officials have no financial incentive to pass the policies that will make our communities whole again. When your campaign coffers depend on the resources of corporations, the accounts are filled only when one's campaign prioritizes the policies that best serve the interests of said institutions. Simply put, money in politics is equivalent to corporations' edicts of quid pro quo.

The average American does not have the resources to impact politics as corporations and the elites who run them do. But millions of people, united behind a legislative agenda that would improves their lives, the lives of their families, and the lives of people in their communities, could be a formidable challenge to corporate power and money in politics. Independent political power works to advance a legislative agenda. When we organize to use our votes and our voices strategically—without making unnecessary compromises—while placing grassroots pressure on corporations and the people who run them, we can lower the impact of corporate money in politics and hold the government accountable to the people it is supposed to serve, instead of to the highest bidder.

Democracy is not a spectator sport—it requires the regular and active participation of the people. Today politics—and the policies that result from it—operate largely in the absence of the people those policies affect. Every day thousands of decisions are being made about us, without us. Yet when health care costs rise, when abortion rights are weakened, or when police departments get yet another infusion of cash from state and federal governments, we are up in arms.

It's not by accident that most of these decisions happen behind closed doors. But even when the doors are open, not many working-class people fill the seats. Though we allegedly live in a democracy, our system is not designed for mass participation. For democracy to survive, that needs to change.

We can preserve democracy and build political power through myriad steps. This includes instituting automatic voter registration as individuals turn eighteen years old, creating people's assemblies with local and state legislators that help to design and inform legislative proposals, and holding workshops for community members to share knowledge about how government works and, more important, how government can work for them.

Right now political parties and candidates alike shirk the responsibility of engagement, leaving the work to underfunded and overworked nonprofit organizations that operate with a fraction of the resources available to political parties, political candidates, and elected officials. Too many elected officials expect their constituents to come to them and make their voices heard, reflecting a fundamental misunderstanding of what it means to represent the people who voted for them.

Within political parties exists an insular culture with an insider dynamic that requires you to know the policies, procedures, and key people in particular positions to make your opinion count. This too represents a fundamental misunderstanding of the role of political parties, which is to organize the communities they represent and engage those communities in setting the agenda.

Furthermore, political parties and elected officials often have weak connections to the community-based organizations that engage local residents around their priorities and concerns. A recalibration of the relationship between and among these entities, and the addition of new strategies for engagement and decision making, would go a long way toward the goal of building and wielding political power—and in building an inclusive democracy.

Another indicator of political power is whether there are consequences when the people you elect to represent you, disappoint you. As Rashad Robinson, president of Color of Change, often says, no one was worried about disappointing Black people when Black people were left stranded on roofs during Hurricane Katrina, surrounded by rising floodwaters because of deep disinvestment in Black communities.[6] President George W. Bush, as he flew over the damage in *Air Force One*, was not worried about disappointing Black people.[7]

Presently, few elected officials or people in positions of institutional power are concerned about the consequences of disappointing Black communities. To change that, Black communities must be organized in such a way that we are concerned less about being seen at the table than about deciding who sits at the table—and under what conditions they are allowed to remain.

To levy consequences, too many choose a posture of non-engagement, mistaking this approach for strategic engagement.

Many choose not to engage in the process, disappointed by the actions or votes of elected officials, or upset or disgusted at the state of politics. They think a hands-off approach is an effective form of resistance. To make matters worse, some might even classify such an action as a boycott of sorts, mirroring the strategic resistance popularized during Dr. King's era.

There are several problems with this perspective. Such nonengagement places hyper-importance on the influence of the individual as opposed to the power of the collective. This is rooted in what I call the fairy tales prevalent in the United States—fairy tales that intentionally distort this country's history and that ultimately discourage the strategic actions that could ameliorate some of our worst societal ills. These stories paint social change as the result of the actions of one person, as opposed to the coordinated and strategic actions of hundreds, thousands, and sometimes millions of people, all moving toward a common goal.

One person's nonparticipation merely results in more room for the opposition to advance unopposed.

Instead, Black communities must organize to levy consequences when our representatives disappoint us. That includes not just taking action to remove someone from office but replacing them with someone who is ready to be held accountable to the community's agenda and not just their own. We must cultivate candidates in this same manner, building a bench of people who are ready to help advance our collective strategy and to achieve justice in all its forms.

Increasing the political power of Black communities is a critical component to building an inclusive democracy in the United States. We must strive to achieve both cultural and policy changes that create the conditions for an equal and just society— and political power is often the missing ingredient for how we get there.

ON BLACK WOMEN'S ELECTORAL POWER

Hon. Crystal Hudson

Following the 2020 U.S. elections, many cable TV commentators wondered, *What if Black women had not saved the Democratic Party?* At the same time, editorials in newspapers across the country devoted pages to lauding the role that Black Americans—particularly Black women—played in delivering the White House and both chambers of Congress to Democrats. This was accomplished despite the stubborn stereotype that Black people don't vote. "Democrats growing anxious—again—over Black turnout," read a headline in *Politico* a week ahead of the 2022 midterm elections.[1]

But what's missing in this lazy narrative is how difficult state governments make it to vote. While Republican-controlled states are proactive in enacting antidemocratic laws, Democratic-controlled states fail to expeditiously pass reforms to strengthen voting rights and encourage more robust civic participation. New York, for example, has outlawed "Wrong Church" ballot disqualification and passed the John R. Lewis Voting Rights Advancement Act, but it doesn't have same-day voter registration or statewide, comprehensive oversight over local election administration. Yet despite the onerous barriers to electoral participation rooted in the country's long history of anti-Black racism, Black Americans *do* vote. Black women especially vote.

And when Black folks vote, we make history. We have offered our nation a lifeline time and time again, despite never once being offered one ourselves. In 2008, Black voter turnout was within one percentage point of white voter turnout, once again delivering Democrats the presidency, electing the nation's first Black president, and securing Democrats the House of Representatives and the Senate. This trend has held over the last decade and is not limited to presidential election years. In 2017 Alabama held a special election for the U.S. Senate seat vacated by Republican Jeff Sessions once he was appointed to be the eighty-fourth U.S. attorney general. Black women in Alabama— making up 17 percent of the electorate—sent Democrat Doug Jones to Washington, D.C., over Republican Roy Moore, as 98 percent of Black women voters cast their ballots for Jones.[2] Jones became the first Democrat to win a U.S. Senate seat in Alabama in twenty-five years.

Taken for granted today by politicians vying for office, Black people's vote has never been guaranteed. It is a struggle that persists, marking our participation in elections as one that is equal parts contemporary survival, civic responsibility, pride, and acknowledgment of the sacrifice that generations of activists— many of whom never saw the fruits of their labor—made to secure suffrage for all marginalized people. A defense of a right too frequently undermined and a privilege rarely neglected, the participation of Black people in the political arena is radical. The saving of American democracy by Black people, and by Black women in particular, is a rich tradition deeply rooted in our struggle to be seen, to be heard, and to be treated equally. It is all in pursuit of an American dream that is more often than not deferred.

The experiences of my late mother, Carole Kay Hudson, made this clear to me. Born in 1941, she came of age at the height of the civil rights movement. She, like her generational peers, was shaped by the work, life, and death of the era's quintessential Black leaders like Medgar Evers, Rev. Dr. Martin Luther King, Jr., and Malcolm X. But she was also inspired by the work of Dorothy Height, Ella Baker, Shirley Chisholm, and many other women who shaped the civil rights movement. At a young age, my mother instilled in me the same conviction that the Black women of the civil rights and woman suffrage movements had instilled in her: Black women are pillars of power, and leveraging that power means exercising our right to vote.

Ever since I can remember, my mother took me to our local elementary school, P.S. 9, a mere two blocks from our home in Brooklyn, to watch her cast her ballot. As a child, I didn't always know who was on the ballot, but I understood the importance of voting. My mother would encourage me to stand close to her, behind the curtain, and place my hand over hers as she pulled down the lever to cast her ballot. It was a lesson not simply in participation but in civic duty and one that I did not take lightly. As I grew older, I became excited and impatient for the opportunity to cast my own ballot. My mother had instilled in me both a civic duty and a genuine excitement to play my part in the exercise of modern democracy. The first presidential election I was eligible to vote in was the contest between George W. Bush and John Kerry in 2004. While it was not one I found to be particularly rousing,

I knew that nothing would keep me from fulfilling my civic duty. Voting had become a point of pride and a family tradition that I valued greatly.

A decade later my mother was diagnosed with Alzheimer's disease, and our roles were reversed—instead of taking me to vote, I now brought her to the polls. My wife and I turned the two-block walk to the same poll site I had visited as a child into a fun family excursion with my mother. Once we greeted the poll workers, I would help her properly fill in the bubbles on the ballot, and we would all get our I VOTED stickers on the way out and take a selfie to commemorate the occasion. And while I took pride in ensuring that my mother could still cast her ballot, our experience reminded me of how burdensome the electoral process can be for older Americans and people with disabilities, with issues ranging from lack of transportation access to frequent changes in polling locations and constitutionally dubious voter identification requirements. Though it was not an issue for us in New York, voter protection groups have warned of the impact that voter ID requirements have on older voters.[3] These are the very people who fostered the communities we live in and who fought for the critical civil rights victories we so often take for granted today.

Yet we cast older Americans aside, making it harder for them to vote and, more broadly, to participate in everyday communal life. The issue of ballot accessibility is especially acute in hard-to-reach rural areas and small cities with significant Black populations. Nevertheless Black voters persist. And in no place is an organized response to systemic disenfranchisement more visible than in our nation's Black churches. Weeks before the 2022 midterm elections, polls projected a weak performance by Democrats in Pennsylvania—a battleground state with a Senate seat and a governorship hanging in the balance. In response, Philadelphia's Black churches galvanized their communities with extensive get-out-the-vote efforts, organizing phonebanks, prayer vigils, and carpools to voting sites.[4] Black churches in Georgia responded similarly, and both states delivered for the Democrats.

The church has long been a site of political power and empowerment for Black people across the nation. Candidates running for office covet time in front of Black churchgoers. Maintaining a congregation's support is even more critical for those who hope to stay in office. However, before the right to vote was extended to Black people, the church was a space for political and social organizing. Churches offered as beacons of hope, messages of freedom and resistance that affirmed parishioners' humanity. More than two hundred years ago the Free African Society—the first recorded Black mutual aid group—was officially secular, but it inspired the creation of the abolitionist African Episcopal Church of St. Thomas.[5] Today Black churches of various denominations continue to use the gospel as a tool toward the achievement of true liberation.

And Black women are at the helm of these institutions. In Washington, D.C., Nannie Helen Burroughs, for example, was a key contributor to the woman suffrage movement, finding in her Black church the space to organize and agitate for change. In a speech to the National Baptist Convention in 1900, Burroughs identified the political power of Black women when she asked Black women churchgoers to "come now to the rescue."[6] With those words, she addressed a whole nation, demanding complete freedom and the right to vote.

Later in the twentieth century, the Student Nonviolent Coordinating Committee, the Congress of Racial Equity, the Black Panther Party, and countless other organizations found a home for social and political organizing in the Black church— organizations whose women members played central, outsize roles.[7] Today the agitators and organizers of yesterday have grown old, but they remain fixtures in our communities and, especially, in our churches. Within the Silent and Baby Boomer generations, nearly two-thirds of Black people report attending a predominantly Black church in their community.[8] The implications carry significant political weight and illustrate the concentration of power in an institution with deep roots in the lives and work of women and older generations. Possessing a unique ability to command thousands of voters, the strength of the Black church lies not solely in those who were its trailblazers and leaders but in its cohesive vision and ability to act in service of a future where it is empowered, and its congregants emboldened.

This legacy is uniquely defined by the contributions of women and other Americans who have seen our country's capacity for change. But we must not rest on our laurels. To deliver for our nation's Black and brown, poor, and working-class populations, we must enact pro-voter reforms. Despite countless obstacles, the power of the Black electorate is routinely on display. The voting process should be simple and convenient. However, long lines, limited voting times, voter roll purges, arbitrary registration requirements, and technological glitches make voting inaccessible to many people in communities of color, in low-income communities, as well as to students and older adults.

Today more than half of the country continues to be without automatic voter registration laws. The federal government must expand early voting to make voting more accessible, it must and set minimum standards for states to meet. We must restore the 1965 Voting Rights Act to its full strength, and all levels of government must address the material needs of Black women. They must do so with the intention of creating more opportunity for all people, especially those who have been systematically pushed to the margins of our society. Beyond electoral reforms, housing guarantees, family-sustaining wages, universal health care, and free college are the path forward.

Those who came before us paved the way to substantive and tangible change, and we can certainly do the same. I serve in the New York City Council, in the same seat previously held by trail-blazing women like Mary Pinkett and Letitia James. They exemplify our capacity to build a better future. In the words of Nannie Helen Burroughs, the country will "find [the Black woman's vote] a tower of strength of which poets have never sung, orators have never spoken, and scholars have never written."[9]

ON EQUITY IN EDUCATION

Hon. Kim Michelle Janey

> It's easier to build strong children than fix broken men.
> —*Frederick Douglass, 1855*

Educational inequality is as American as apple pie. Inequality is built into the nation's educational system.[1] The country's origin story reveals who was considered worthy of an education: white men. Many believed that an educated citizenry was necessary to ensure the nascent nation's growth and prosperity. The country's first public school was founded in Boston in 1635, long before independence. Six years later Massachusetts became the very first colony to legalize slavery.

Being born into a family of educators has helped shape who I am and the work that I have done throughout my career. I understand the importance of high-quality education and how it can change the trajectory and life outcomes for children living in poverty. As a five-year-old, I attended a Black independent community school organized and led by Black parents; at eleven, I

experienced the trauma of court ordered busing; and later I grad-
uated from a better-funded white school in the suburbs through
a voluntary busing program. My personal journey has informed
my work as an education advocate. I later fought for systemic policy changes that expanded educational opportunity and addressed
achievements gaps.

I took this fight to the Boston City Council, where I advocated for greater teacher diversity, increased dual language opportunities, improved vocational and technical opportunities, and
equal access to prestigious schools. Forty-five years after surviving
the tumultuous bussing era, I became mayor of Boston, respon-
sible for safely reopening schools that had been closed due to the
COVID-19 pandemic and managing the distribution of millions
of dollars of federal relief. After more than twenty years advocating for racial equity policies and systemic change, I now had
the ability to implement them from the highest office in the city.
Even during my short tenure, I made historic appointments to the
Boston School Committee that improved language access, and I
changed how students are assigned to the city's three exam schools,
including Boston Latin School, the nation's oldest public school.

I knew from experience that quality education is not only a
pathway to productive citizenship and individual success but also
a way to strengthen families and transform communities. My
work has always been deeply rooted in the belief that parents must
be treated as respected partners in their children's education. Over
the years, parents and students increasingly have developed their
own voices in the fight for equity and quality education.

This fight is not a new one. Throughout U.S. history, Black
people have always had to fight for quality education.[2] In 1848
five-year-old Sarah Roberts was assigned to an inferior segregated
school for Black children in Boston. When her father tried enrolling her in the local school that was closer to home but reserved

for white students, she was forcibly removed by a police officer. Sarah's father filed a lawsuit. In 1850 the Massachusetts Supreme Court's ruling upheld racial segregation, and legal Jim Crow was born in the city of Boston. The Massachusetts court's ruling was the precursor and precedent for codifying "separate but equal" in the 1896 Supreme Court decision *Plessy v. Ferguson*.

"Separate but equal" would be the law of the land, until the 1954 *Brown v. Board of Education* Supreme Court case argued for the plaintiffs by Thurgood Marshall, who would later become the first African American appointed to serve on that body. The groundbreaking 1954 ruling determined that racial segregation in public schools was unconstitutional.

While Boston takes pride in its abolitionist history, it has struggled to live up to those ideals. In 1965, nine years after *Brown v. Board of Education*, Massachusetts established the Racial Imbalance Act in an effort to desegregate schools. This gave the state's Board of Education the authority to investigate and reduce racial imbalances in public schools. A school was determined to be racially imbalanced if 50 percent or more of its students were students of color. Not surprisingly, schools that were predominantly Black were assigned less qualified teachers and received fewer resources.[3]

I attended New School for Children, a Black independent community school, born out of the Black liberation movement of the 1960s. This school had a majority of students of color by design. One of the things I remember most about my two years at the school is the way it made me feel. They were feelings that my five-year-old self could not put into words. I felt seen. I felt connected to people who were not only like me but also cared for me. I also felt safe.

But that would be short-lived. In 1974, twenty years after the *Brown v. Board of Education* ruling, Judge W. Arthur Garrity issued a desegregation order for the Boston public schools. School buses would transport Black children to white schools in white neighborhoods and white children to schools that were predominantly Black.

In 1976, now enrolled in public school, I was bused to a white working-class neighborhood, where we were greeted every day with racial slurs, rocks, sticks, and cans. Our school buses often had to be escorted by the police. Almost fifty years later, the public schools in Boston are still segregated by race, and families are still desperately seeking and demanding a quality education for their children.

As with many movements for racial justice, Black women were at the forefront of the fight for quality education in Boston. Black women like Ruth Baston, Ellen Jackson, Julia Walker, Jean McGuire, and so many others organized and advocated for equity in education. Yet they will never appear in a history textbook. And even if their stories are told, given the current political climate, there's still a chance that schoolchildren would not have access to that material.

Today the challenges are many. Public schools do not have the resources they need to meet the varied needs of our diverse student population. Special education students, especially Black and Latino boys, are often isolated from their peers in substantially separate classrooms. In addition, school discipline and exclusion from the classroom disproportionately impact Black students.

Too frequently schools are ill-prepared to receive immigrant children who speak languages other than English, especially those whose formal education may have been interrupted before they arrived in the United States. The same is true for students experiencing trauma.

While there have been investments in social emotional wellness over the years, nothing could have prepared us for the COVID-19 pandemic and the lasting impact that it has had on our children. Students experienced the personal loss of loved ones as well as learning loss. Teachers, parents, and students should be applauded for their commitment to push through with remote learning, but nothing can take the place of physically being in the classroom with one's teachers and peers.

Prior to the pandemic, families were already having a difficult time making ends meet. As we seek to correct bad policies and replace them with new ones, we cannot ignore the harm that the pandemic has created in our schools. Children who were already experiencing racial opportunity gaps before the pandemic are now experiencing even larger educational divides. The pandemic laid bare the inequities in our public education system, exposing and exacerbating challenges that were already there.

This is a critical time in our nation's history. Its legacy of inequality is threatening our future workforce and is tearing away at the fabric of our democracy. At more than 245 years old, our democracy is tattered like a weatherbeaten flag. The foundational principles of freedom of speech and of thought are now viewed as threats rather than as the cornerstones that keep our democracy strong. The refusal of some local and state governments to even acknowledge race or racism does not absolve them from their responsibility to create fair and just policies. Government must be held accountable for creating equitable opportunities and for dismantling systems that exacerbate and perpetuate racial inequities. This problem is bigger than any one individual or political party.

The racial inequities evident in public education are a product of a system of white supremacy built on a foundation of chattel slavery—a system that was deliberately and methodically crafted by the first colonists, institutionalized by the founding fathers, and perfected by subsequent generations of lawmakers. A four-hundred-year-old system will not crumble easily. Dismantling it will take political will and hard work. It will require all of us to work together, including those who benefit from that very system.

So where do we go from here? What are the solutions? As dire as things may sound, there is hope. That same activist spirit of generations past is alive and well. We can ensure that students have the resources and tools they need to thrive. We need bold, courageous leadership that is willing to invest in our children and make the necessary changes to improve educational outcomes for all children, regardless of race, ethnicity, language, immigration status, religion, gender identity or expression, special needs, or zip code.

Instead of preparing the next generation of leaders, this nation invests more in its prisoners than it does in its pupils. As Frederick Douglass reminds us, we either pay for the investment on the front end, or we pay for the lack of investment and risk losing a generation of children.

We have to define what it means to give our students a quality education. If the definition of quality education is one that perpetuates racism and white supremacy, we will never dismantle the school-to-prison pipeline. We can just look to the national discourse in American politics for evidence of how much work we must do to eliminate racism from our society, including its educational system.

In order to repair the harm of centuries of inequality in education, we must make strategic investments that ensure a high-quality cadre of educators, state-of-the-art facilities, and decolonized curricula that do not center European history. Our students must be prepared to compete in a global economy, and they should be exposed to the history of people of color in the United States and throughout the world.

An investment in educators must include strategies to recruit, hire, develop, and retain a highly qualified, diverse cadre of teach-

ers. Educators should be held accountable for reducing opportunity gaps, and they must be supported to do their jobs well.
The focus on educators must also include recruiting more men of
color into the classroom, especially Black and Latino male teachers, and more teachers with linguistic diversity—expanding dual
language not only for English learners but for all students.

Building a more inclusive democracy that protects the rights
and freedom of all means investing in our children and in their
families. The growing income divide coupled with the lack of
affordable housing has put a strain on poor families living in urban
communities. Families in rural communities are also stretched to
their limit financially. Everyone deserves to earn a living wage, so
that they can not just survive but thrive.

Families want to live where there are great parks, homes, businesses, schools, and a strong sense of community. Poor families
are often left to struggle in neighborhoods that may be rich in
nonprofits and human service organizations, but these organizations may not be providing support and services to help lift families out of poverty. Families need the tools and support to climb
the economic ladder. When families are happier and healthier,
students have better outcomes.

Most Americans believe we live in a nation where achieving
their dreams is possible, regardless of race, gender, class, religion,
sexuality, zip code, or immigration status. I don't believe we are
there yet, but we should strive to make it a reality. Perfecting our
Union is ongoing work. The vision moving forward must be one
that promotes and protects the true liberation of Black Americans
after four hundred years of oppression. It can be realized only
when we work toward true freedom and justice for all, including
those who have historically been left out of the American dream.

So how do we get there? What is the most effective strategy
to realize the vision? I often think back to the Black women in

my community growing up. Black women stood in the gap and became a bridge for Black children to cross. Our communities are filled with Black women who have been doing the work as unsung heroes. More and more Black women are being recognized for their leadership. And more and more Black women are running for public office.

Women generally lead differently. They are thoughtful and strategic. They know how to multitask and focus on the greater good over personal gain. They are resilient, in part because they've had to be. Racism and sexism are ever present, but Black women persevere. They often bring a unique combination of skills and qualifications that make them ideal leaders in politics and other sectors.

To enact new legislation and policies that can begin to repair the harm that has resulted from educational inequality, we need more Black women running for elected office, from school boards to city halls and especially to Congress. As I have often said, Black women are saving this country one election at a time. The challenges in our country cannot be resolved in one election cycle. There's no magic pill, no quick fix to build an inclusive democracy. However, we can take some steps forward. We must focus on equity and inclusion and on dismantling systemic racism. We must continue to put forth an agenda that creates real opportunities for everyone, not just for a select few. And most of all, we must continue this fight for freedom and justice for all.

ON FREEDOM FROM POLICING

Mariame Kaba

W e're in the midst of yet another bipartisan crime panic. Democratic mayors in San Francisco, Chicago, D.C., Atlanta, and New York City are loudly demanding "law and order" while President Joe Biden calls for 100,000 more police officers on the streets.[1] On the right, Republicans stoke conspiracy theories about a border crisis in which immigrants are flooding the nation with drugs, diseases, and, of course, crime. Across the political spectrum, lawmakers urge us to be afraid of strangers, of our neighbors, and of each other.

The drumbeat of fear is hyperbolic and manipulative. It's effective, though, because most of the people who live in the United States do not feel safe most of the time. By all reasonable measures, ours is a violent and dangerous society.

The United States has more than ten times the number of

gun homicides than most comparable countries. Our rates of childhood gun deaths are terrifyingly high, and even more panic inducing, they are increasing.[2] Our health care system has gaping holes; 27.5 million people still lack health insurance.[3] Our maternal mortality rates are more than twice as high as those of peer countries; Black maternal mortality rates are more than four times as high.[4] Homelessness is rising.[5] Life expectancy is falling.[6] And the United States has had a dismal pandemic response compared to countries with similar resources.[7]

When people are scared, they want security. Police and prisons seem like an answer. Police can arrest "bad guys" carrying firearms. They can sweep the homeless out of sight, so the general public isn't reminded of their own precariousness.

Yet even though the United States has 2 million people behind bars and the highest incarceration rate in the world, Americans still don't feel safe.[8] In fact, policing simply creates more precarity and fear, especially in marginalized communities. Studies show that Black people are five to ten times more likely to be arrested than white peers.[9] Almost half of Black men, and 40 percent of white men, are arrested at least once by age twenty-three.[10] Being constantly threatened with arrest and imprisonment makes people feel less secure, not more protected.

And when people feel less secure, politicians offer more police.

Safety is a rhetorical weapon wielded to make people feel less safe. We are in an endless cycle of fear, which generates an authoritarian reaction, generating more fear and more authoritarian reaction. *How do we break free?*

What does the term *safety* mean in particular for me, a Black Muslim woman born to return migrant parents in the United States? I often come back to a James Baldwin quote:

Nobody knows what is going to happen to him from one moment to the next, or how one will bear it. This is irreducible. And it's true of everybody. Now, it is true that the nature of society is to create, among its citizens, an illusion of safety; but it is also absolutely true that the safety is always necessarily an illusion.[11]

To say that safety is illusory is not to say that it isn't a valid and real need. Instead, it is to acknowledge that safety is not something that I can possess in a permanent, personal way. Safety isn't a thing: it's a social relation. I'm more or less safe depending on my relationship to others and to my proximity to the resources I need to survive.

If you ask me today if I feel more or less safe, my answer will depend on different factors. Did I get paid today? Scarcity, after all, is a type of violence; if I can't pay rent, I will feel unsafe. Did I log on to the internet today and see stories of missing white women and mass shootings? Do I have people I can lean on if some calamity befalls me, or do I feel alone? The truth is that we co-create safety through trusting relationships.

Policing is touted as a solution to all insecurity. But police are themselves a threat. Moreover, police encourage us to see safety in division. They are focused on cordoning off "wrongdoers" based on race, class, sexuality, gender, and respectability. A main consequence of policing is to separate people. But separating people works to separate us from what does provide a sense of stability, and hope, as well as safety—which is the support of others.

This may seem counterintuitive. We've been conditioned to seeing other people as threats that need to be managed, controlled, and policed. Without police, movies and politicians constantly tell us, we would descend into a violent war of all against all.

The truth, however, is that when you remove police, people don't attack each other. They build community. In *A Paradise Built in Hell*, writer Rebecca Solnit examines a range of natural and man-made disasters throughout history. What she finds is that when faced with sweeping catastrophes, people's first instinct is to help each other.[12] In a similar vein, activist Dorothy Day was transformed by the experience of the 1906 San Francisco earthquake. Reflecting on it thirty years later, she noted, "What I remember most plainly about the earthquake was the human warmth and kindliness of everyone afterward. . . . While the crisis lasted, people loved each other."[13]

During disasters, police and government are often slow to arrive and slow to respond. When they do arrive on the scene, they often make things worse rather than better. For example, they're often focused on stopping people from taking desperately needed supplies from stores (so-called looting). Sometimes authorities themselves engage in looting or attack those trying to help each other. There is a double standard around what appropriation, and by whom, both police and media understand as "looting." The solidarity in disasters—the revelation that people don't actually need police—is often seen by authorities as a threat, and they react accordingly.

Disasters are, by definition, very unsafe. But for that very reason, they break the cycle of safety politics. When people recognize they have little to lose, they are free to let go of mutual fear and act as if they care for one another.

Waiting for an earthquake is obviously not much of a plan for change. But you don't have to have an apocalypse to try to build safety *with* neighbors rather than in spite of them.

In 2010 I was living in an apartment building in Chicago where music kept me awake every night into the early morning hours. Alleys in the city often double as hangout spots for teens. Young people would party by the building until someone called the police. The police would arrive and tell the teens to go away, or else arrest them for curfew violations. And the next night the whole cycle would repeat.

I had founded Project NIA a year earlier to address youth criminalization. I knew that for young people, encounters with police are traumatic and can escalate dangerously. I also have insomnia, and loud noise at two a.m. was leaving me, and everyone else in the apartment complex, exhausted.

So I tried to find another solution. I met with neighbors and suggested inviting the teens to lunch to talk about the issue.

My neighbors were understandably anxious. A lunch might make things worse; a teen might act out and become violent. I offered to talk to them myself, and eventually we arranged a meal with five teens and two neighbors. My neighbors explained that the noise was disruptive, and that there were small children in the apartment building who were being kept awake. The teens explained that they were playing the music loudly because they had been "disrespected." A neighbor had threatened to call the cops without giving them a chance to turn the music down. Once we apologized to them, they agreed to stop playing the music so loudly.

The police were not the solution. They were the problem; turning to the police to fix the situation had only escalated it. It was only when the community reached out—without the police—that the situation could be resolved.

This illustrates what prison industrial complex (PIC) abolitionists like myself argue—that police are a barrier to conflict resolution. If you care about the violence of policing, then you should want as little policing as possible in any form. If we want to move toward a more caring, less violent society, we need to immediately shrink police power and to redirect resources to life-affirming needs. This is the essence of the call to #DefundPolicing.

Defunding police prevents the police from terrorizing and harassing marginalized people. And it also makes funds available to invest in education, health care, and community building, creating a sense of trust and stability.

Currently, police budgets take up a huge share of city resources.[14] Baltimore for example, spends 26 percent of its budget on policing; Miami spends 33 percent; Chicago spends *37 percent.* Yet there's no evidence that police spending reduces crime.[15]

In contrast, research has shown that more spending on social services is strongly correlated with reduction in homicide rates.[16] Investment in public schools as well as spending on social welfare has also been shown to decrease crime.[17] Community-based violence interruption programs, which provide funds for respected members of the community to build personal relationships with people at the center of violence, have also been effective.[18]

Spending a third or more of a city's budget on police doesn't leave much to fund the approaches that do reduce violence. Police starve civil society of the resources that could be used to address real problems. That leads to greater insecurity and fear, which police then use to argue that they need even *more* money.

Defunding police, therefore, isn't just about reducing police budgets. It's about working toward the project of "a social life lived differently" by organizing for abolitionist safety.

One current site of struggle is Seattle. Abolitionist organizers have issued a call for a budget—the Seattle Solidarity Budget—that "centers the needs of the most marginalized and vulnerable."[19] They have focused on the rising numbers of deaths in King County Jail and among homeless people targeted by police for removal.

This is an example of solidarity in practice, with more than two hundred community groups supporting the proposed budget. "At the core of the Solidarity Budget is our refusal to allow our movements to be pitted against each other for funding," the organization's website states. "Divesting from police systems and investing in Black communities goes hand in hand with climate justice work and housing justice work and participatory budgeting."[20]

The Solidarity Budget is an example of real and substantive democracy as opposed to the cramped and hollow sort to which we are accustomed. The coalition has had some successes; it cut Seattle's police budget by $11 million and expanded investments in affordable housing, community services, and transit.[21] Its ultimate demands include a 50 percent cut in the Seattle Police Department's budget, dramatic climate action, and an investment in good jobs and community resilience.[22]

What I deeply appreciate about the Seattle Solidarity Budget is that it does what I think we most need: convening people across communities and sectors to have robust conversations and to make decisions about what those communities most value and want.

The work has been grueling. Police, politicians, and reactionaries have made efforts to derail the initiative. There has also been internal conflict among members of the coalition. Yet organizers and community members are pressing on and persisting. They are showing us that *organizing is the how*. It's how we get from where we are to where we want to go. Black freedom movement organizer Ella Baker taught us this.

Scholar and activist Ruth Wilson Gilmore argues that the rise of the carceral state is the result of the underdevelopment of the social welfare state.[23] I think the rise of the carceral state is also the *cause* of the underdevelopment of the social welfare state. Disinvestment in education, in health care, and in democracy leads to more policing. More policing in turn feeds on the rest of society like a giant bloated mosquito with a badge.

This is why police reform is a perpetuation of the problem rather than a solution to it. Reforms assume that the police are a fundamentally effective and democratic institution. Reformers believe that if you could just tweak the police, they would stop lying in reports and depositions.[24] They would cease shooting unarmed Black people. They might even somehow miraculously start preventing crimes. And so reformers look to body cameras (which police turn off when they feel like it) or to civilian oversight boards (which police often block or neuter) or to training, which has little effect on police use of violence.[25]

Most reforms involve giving the police more resources—training and body cameras cost money. Thus, they end up perpetuating the real problem, which is that ineffective, violent policing uses up all the resources that could be used for effective, nonviolent approaches.

Policing is a practice, but it's also a tactic and a vision. The carceral state is built on the principle that Black people, poor people, and other marginalized people are the cause of insecurity and that they must be detained, walled off, and tormented if others are to enjoy a good life of safety and affluence. The fact that the carceral state does not actually provide safety is not a failure but the point of its existence. The goal is ever-escalating fear, providing forever escalating punishment and hate. A police state is a state that wants to police more, and more fiercely. It is fundamentally opposed to freedom and solidarity. It is designed to build walls.

Many of those walls are in our heads. During a virtual teach-in in 2020, writer Patrick Blanchfield said that the police "are in our minds as a solution rather than as a problem." Whenever PIC abolitionists call for the elimination of policing, people immediately and aggressively push back by insisting that we provide "an alternative" to address public safety. The question hurled at us is "Well what will replace the police?" They should ask instead, what are police replacing? Or as Chicago-based organizer Damon Williams put it, "When I see police, I see 100 other jobs smashed into one thing with a gun."[26]

If policing is the solution, that doesn't leave any room for the rest of us to have influence. The (alleged) expertise of police leaves no room for decision making by the public at large—not to mention that the notion of "crime" constructs large swaths of the public as unworthy of anything but violence. It undermines any notion of democracy.

We don't know what our nation without police would look like. But we know that our society with police is violent, racist, precarious, unequal, and unfree. The carceral state is a choice. Abolitionists believe that if we work, dream, and imagine together, we can choose something else.

ON ECONOMIC JUSTICE

Hon. Nina Turner

We specialize in the wholly impossible.
—*Nannie Helen Burroughs*

It always seems impossible until it is done.
—*Nelson Mandela*

In 1966, A. Philip Randolph, one of the most prominent labor leaders of the twentieth century, led a group of economists and activists in creating a framework to address the political and economic systems' failures that had continually crushed the hopes and dreams of Black people and working-class people in the United States. Entitled *A "Freedom Budget" for All Americans*, the primary aim of the plan was to eradicate poverty by 1975. To attain "true" freedom, Randolph and his associates argued that Americans needed an ironclad social contract steeped in economic justice and human rights. Each person and family would have a strong financial foundation, one that guaranteed basic necessities to all, including food, clothing, and shelter. To that end, the major pillars of the budget included promises of full employment, an adequate minimum wage, a decent home for every American family, modern health care services for all, and full educational opportunities.[1]

At the time this budget was being drafted, the Vietnam War was raging, and federal officials were prioritizing funds to meet the growing demands of the conflict. It was almost unfathomable that they would consider enacting A "Freedom Budget" for All Americans.

Conservative politicians savvily pointed out that resources were limited. They insisted that rising poverty could be sorted out once the war was over. Other naysayers—let's call them the practical, pragmatic crew—called the budget too ambitious. They chose not to focus on the conditions that created the need for such a robust plan in the first place.[2]

Thankfully, the authors of A "Freedom Budget" for All Americans moved forward with preparing the plan. Randolph took the criticisms head on in the document's introduction. "Those drafting this Freedom Budget," he explained, "have sought to outline, objectively and fully, the steps required for the abolition of poverty in America." "It may be argued that the Freedom Budget is too ambitious to be politically feasible," he continued. "We contend that the proper question is whether the persistence of poverty is any longer feasible."[3]

With these words, Randolph asked the naysayers to shift their perspective. He challenged them to focus on the people who needed a policy shift of this magnitude. He went on to ask a profound, rhetorical question that illustrated the need for his plan: "How many examples of seething discontent do we need before we move earnestly to provide jobs for all, clear the slums, rebuild our cities, overcome shortages of schools and hospitals, and reverse the neglect of our other social needs?"[4] Randolph refused to allow detractors to stop him from addressing the needs of the poor during the 1960s and '70s. He and his associates not only identified the problem but also offered solutions. They called on the federal government to institute fundamental policies that would lift Americans out of poverty.

Approximately two hundred American activists endorsed *A "Freedom Budget" for All Americans.* A diverse group of Black leaders—such as Dorothy Height of the National Council of Negro Women, Rev. Dr. Martin Luther King, Jr., of the Southern Christian Leadership Conference, Stokely Carmichael of the Student Nonviolent Coordinating Committee, and actors Ruby Dee and Ossie Davis—supported this revolutionary agenda. This impressively broad coalition alone underscored the urgency of the moment. Eager to find ways to ameliorate the challenges facing impoverished and working-class people, these Black leaders shared a bold and unapologetic vision of economic justice.

While Randolph and his collaborators introduced *A "Freedom Budget" for All Americans* during the 1960s, the proposal built on the New Deal programs that had been introduced by President Franklin Delano Roosevelt several decades before. The Great Depression and World War II deeply shaped President Roosevelt's perspectives on poverty. He recognized that winning the global war against fascism required collaboration with other nations as well as a firm commitment to addressing the material needs of the American people. Taking a dual approach—attending to both global and domestic affairs—was a necessary step to cultivating lasting peace.

During his State of the Union address on January 11, 1944, President Roosevelt argued that survival alone was insufficient. "I do not think that any of us Americans can be content with mere survival," he explained. "Sacrifices that we and our allies are making impose upon us all a sacred obligation to see to it that out of this war we and our children will gain something better than mere survival."[5] The "sacred obligation" he referenced was the building blocks of what Roosevelt named "a second Bill of Rights."[6] Although the president's plan was visionary, it did not go far enough in recognizing and advancing racial justice especially for Black Americans. A. Philip Randolph and his colleagues during the 1960s, therefore, worked to significantly expand the programs of Roosevelt's era. *A "Freedom Budget" for All Americans* helped to create a moral, political, and economic framework.

There is an overwhelming need to return to *A "Freedom Budget" for All Americans* in the twenty-first century. We will never be able to fully dismantle racism, sexism, and other social ills until every American has access to the foundational rights of quality health care, income and job security, housing, education without mountains of debt, and other resources that improve the quality of life. We have an obligation and an opportunity to build an inclusive democracy where economic justice flourishes.

A "Freedom Budget" for All Americans provides a solid foundation on which to build. To make this vision a reality, we must first reimagine what is possible. This calls for shifting our perspective from a scarcity-driven mindset—where we overemphasize "limited" resources—to an abundance-driven mindset. This shift is necessary for the advancement of a civil society—and the survival of democratic nations. The formation of a bold, people-centered agenda will usher in an abundance of possibilities. Getting to the crux of those possibilities will require sacrifice, careful planning, and persistence. For far too long we have accepted an image of justice devoid of struggle. We often glorify the victories and overlook the tensions and turmoil that paved the way.

The demands of *A "Freedom Budget" for All Americans* are relevant for the economic needs of today; that so little has changed for impoverished and working-class Americans since the 1960s underscores the urgency of this proposal. Sixty-three percent of Americans today are living paycheck to paycheck.[7] This is disturbing but not surprising considering that the federal minimum wage of $7.25 per hour has not changed since 2009. Many Americans hold multiple jobs simply to make ends meet, which impedes any opportunity for them to have a robust quality of life.[8] Millions of people in the United States have no guaranteed income, and they work without any family medical leave or health care benefits.[9] The overturning of *Roe v. Wade* by an activist right-wing Supreme Court has only worsened conditions, stripping women of their bodily autonomy and therefore placing their reproductive health at risk. This reckless move by the Supreme Court has triggered GOP-led extremist state legislatures to limit women's access to abortion care and other reproductive support. In addition, the Child Tax Credit, created during the COVID-19 pandemic, expired and catapulted so many of our children back into poverty.[10] A new set of policies can—and must—be implemented to enhance the quality of life for all Americans. Poverty is a policy choice. We can choose to dismantle it—it only requires our political will.

If we are truly committed to the ideals of democracy, we must support policies that ensure economic justice for all Americans. This requires holding ourselves—and this country—accountable for this forward and ever-evolving movement toward a just and liberating society. We must make clear, concise demands to leaders, at all levels of government and in every sphere of influence, assuring them that they will face consequences at the polls for not meeting our demands. And nestled in those demands must be a searing belief that a moral-political economy is something that all Americans deserve. We cannot demand it if we do not believe that we deserve it.

We also must not fall so in love with leaders, especially elected leaders, that we fail to critique them when progress stalls. To the contrary, we must insist that our elected officials answer to the needs of people all over the nation—including those living in

some of the most destitute areas. We must reevaluate the markers of progress on a consistent basis. We must work to ensure
that progress is not slow-rolled into a maelstrom of mediocrity
released at a tantalizing tempo to create the illusion of progress
without substance. We must not be seduced by dizzying rhetoric
and pretty faces in high places.

Over the past several years, I have had the opportunity to be
on the national frontlines of efforts to fight for public policies that
would enhance the lives of millions. One such opportunity came
in the form of working on both of Senator Bernie Sanders's (D-
VT) presidential campaigns—in 2016 and 2020—as a national
co-chair and running for Congress in the 2021 (special election)
and 2022 election cycles. Both experiences cemented my deep-
seated belief and commitment to racial, social, and economic justice. As I traveled all over the country, I witnessed firsthand the
impact of neglect and callous indifference to the suffering of poor
people. It was clear to me that the economic system of this nation
was failing our most vulnerable communities, from poisoned
water in Flint, Michigan; Denmark, South Carolina; and Jackson,
Mississippi, to underfunded schools and the lack of affordable
and widely accessible health care for all Americans, This failure
was not by accident—it was by design.

All hope is not lost, however. All this can be re-engineered,
and we have the power to do it. Building an inclusive democracy
requires building an inclusive economy. There is no democracy
without economic freedom. Building a solid coalition around
our collective struggles and having concrete solutions is just as
important today as it was during the 1960s when A. Philip Randolph and his colleagues came together to draft A *"Freedom Budget" for All Americans.*

A vision of a future that saves, satisfies, and sustains is more
than possible. It is transcendent. The words of civil rights pio-

neer and educator Nannie Helen Burroughs informs the mission that lies ahead of us: "To struggle and battle and overcome and absolutely defeat every force designed against us is the only way to achieve."[11] As Black women, we stand at the vanguard of this magnificent mission, and we must be vigilant and present in the crusade to secure economic justice for all Americans. Failure is not an option. It will take a convergence of forces—and collaborations among Americans of diverse backgrounds—to realize the beautiful vision of "freedom from want." To make this vision a reality, it is worth waging a battle against the status quo—the neoliberal incrementalism that has landed us in the immoral, economic wilderness now ravaging our communities. When Black women move, we shake and shape the world. Achievement awaits us!

Part III

COMBATING HATE

ON ANTI-BLACKNESS

Charlene A. Carruthers

We reject pedestals, queenhood, and walking ten paces behind. To be recognized as human, levelly human, is enough.

—Combahee River Collective Statement

Anti-Blackness is a globalized system of beliefs and practices that destroy, erode, and dictate against the humanity of Black people.[1] It is a quotidian and ingrained feature of governance in the United States practiced, albeit at varying degrees, by people across racial groups. Daily practices of control include, but are not limited to, the policing and surveillance sanctioned by state and societal governing institutions that have consistently segmented Black people outside the category of full citizenship and democratic processes.

The development of anti-Blackness through processes of imperialism, settler colonialism, and chattel slavery determines how people live in relation to each other, namely who is considered human and not human. This is true even today. While this development began long before the nation was established, the United States is the site where anti-Blackness developed through so-called democratic processes. White men who colonized this land wrote and voted on legislation that dictated who was enslaved and who was not. Presidents enslaved Africans and their descendants. Enslavers committed acts of sexual violence, neglect, and a variety of physical and emotional brutalities against the people they enslaved. With few exceptions, such as loosely enforced anti-miscegenation laws, the violence was legal through so-called democratic processes.

Anti-Blackness is a phenomenon that transcends a distinct historical moment. It is produced and reproduced over time, always in relation to the past and present. Endeavoring to pin down the moment of its origin diminishes the scope of its genealogy. Instead, the moments in which white European clergy, philosophers, and merchants dictated who was human and who would be categorized as the "Other" are rhizomatic and sprawling.[2]

Anti-Blackness has always been a key feature of governance to maintain power for some and withhold power from others. Just as Black people throughout the Americas refused, resisted, and revolted against anti-Black violence, non-Black people have also reaped rewards through social, political, and economic power.

The daily indignities inflicted by anti-Black systems in the United States persist in federal, state, and municipal laws that enforce educational, housing, employment, food, medical, and political apartheid today. They also persist in the seemingly constant harassment, assault, and killing of Black people viewed by millions in videos captured by bystanders and police body cameras.

Transforming our ways of being and the ways we relate to each other requires much more than reform. Making such deep changes requires a continued movement toward abolishing all systems of oppression. It requires institutions across the nation to shift their agendas. This long-term strategy, as abolitionist Ruth Wilson Gilmore argues, requires that we change one thing: *everything*.[3]

I often return to the work of radical Black feminist activists, community organizers, and writers to sharpen my understanding of what needs to be done. I look to them for guidance on how to do the political, cultural, and educational work needed to actualize transformation. Black feminist thought and action help me make sense of today's world, its history, and can offer wisdom on how to move forward. Writing about their lives and the conditions in which Black people across gender, class, sexuality, and geography encountered violence, Black feminists advance ideas and action that expose and analyze the interiority of Black life.[4]

Throughout the twentieth century, Black women in the United States conducted their "politics in the cracks," as one activist told historian Kimberly Springer.[5] The hidden nature of their political work, also referred to as interstitial politics, held two meanings for Black feminists. According to Springer, Black women found ways to "fit their activism into their daily life schedules whenever possible." They also "developed a collective identity and basis for organizing that reflected the intersecting nature of Black womanhood."[6]

Black feminists created organizations and influenced the political agendas of already existing organizations. By claiming Black feminism as a heterogeneous political identity, Springer argues that Black women activists and organizers "enacted interstitial politics focused on articulating their race, gender, and class identities as interconnected."[7] While tensions, conflicts, challenges, and breakdowns of organizations sometimes occurred, Black feminist organizations were political formations where Black feminists could struggle across class, sexuality, faith, and ideological differences. They were sites where Black feminists practiced governance within a broader society where they were often shut out of mainstream politics.

Black feminists also generated intellectual thought outside formal organizations. Writers such as Ntozake Shange, Toni Cade Bambara, Michele Wallace, Toni Morrison, and Alice Walker published works that were influenced by and that in turn influenced Black feminist organizing. Black feminist thought and action were not solely in the realm of political campaigns agitating politicians and institutions. Their writings sparked public debates within Black communities, particularly among Black men and Black women, about misogyny in movements, institutions, the home, and interpersonal relationships. Popular publications including *Ebony*, *Encore*, and *The Black Scholar* brought debates about Black women and feminism to the public sphere.

The Combahee River Collective, a Black feminist group in Boston during the 1970s, took on these debates directly in their political organizing and intellectual work. The Combahee River Collective Statement, written by Black lesbian feminists Demita Frazier, Beverly Smith, and Barbara Smith in 1977, and first published in 1978, has shaped Black feminism in the United States. The statement offered a concise articulation of interlocking oppressions and identity politics as well as their refusal of a gender separatist feminism and their unapologetic commitment to socialism.[8]

Among the many political commitments and values it articulated, the statement was grounded in the idea of being human, anti-royal, and worthy of liberation. Its framers offered a structural analysis and scenario for dismantling all systems of oppression by asserting that "if Black women were free, it would mean that everyone else would have to be free since our freedom would necessitate the destruction of all the systems of oppression."[9] This statement described the interconnectivity of all oppressed people affected by white supremacy, capitalism, and patriarchy. It is not a statement of a hierarchy of oppression or prioritization of structural problems to address; it demonstrates a political commitment grounded in Black feminist thought and organized action.

The statement further declared that as "Black women we find any type of biological determinism a particularly dangerous and reactionary basis upon which to build a politic." In so doing, it foregrounded contemporary, critical deconstructions of gender binarism within Black studies that address gender, gender identity, and gender performance.[10] As we continue to witness and experience various organized efforts to further marginalize transgender and gender nonconforming people across the country, this declaration is timely and instructive.

Together with other Black feminist organizations, the Combahee River Collective shaped how scholars in Black studies now interrogate gender and sexuality, including queer politics and movements in the United States. Their 1978 statement outlined a vision that surpassed a politics of inclusion in a society where Black women are maligned and leveraged as agents to expand the U.S. colonial project.

Inclusion for the sake of simply being at the table is insufficient and ineffective in today's world. We must refuse to accept representation and presence as markers of power. When a Black woman—or a person of any gender—is elected to political office, we should always pause and ask about the individual's platform and record. Identity does not dictate politics. Every individual's political values and practices are determined by opportunities and choices. Politics, like love, must be backed up by actions.

How do we, as a nation, build the type of governance that advances access to dignity for all people? History and contemporary dynamics reveal that rights and freedoms are never guaranteed for Black people living in the United States. They are always fought for and won through collective struggle. Ongoing attacks on—and the outright stripping of—voting rights have required broad coalitions to organize for the maintenance and expansion of what is often considered the most basic aspect of any functioning democracy. Formerly incarcerated people are at the forefront of this work, and in turn, they expose the need to restore and expand rights and end discrimination against people with convictions.[11]

For a fully functioning democracy to have a chance, we need to move beyond the electoral process. A culture shift from a small number of people holding major decision-making power—including the president of the United States and the Supreme Court—is necessary. Decision making can and must become participatory. It is antidemocratic to allow the few who can fundraise and make the time to run for office have the individual power to make decisions with broad implications for the many. Participatory budgeting—a democratic process in which residents decide how public funds should be spent at the local level—should be standard practice. Participatory budgeting increases community engagement, collective accountability, and spending that reflects the needs of marginalized communities.[12]

If Black women are to be included in anything, it should be a radically transformed system of governance that recognizes the United States as a settler colonial project and also has a sharp commitment to not furthering the spirit of dehumanization. For the United States to be a democracy, it must discontinue dominating and preventing other nations from exercising their own democratic practices. Historical ideas of democracy that are rooted in or even inspired by the idea of the Founding Fathers must go. Until the truth of how anti-Blackness shapes this nation is accepted, we will continue to paint over pain—and fail to build a society based on human dignity and respect for all.

ON ANTI-LGBTQ+ VIOLENCE

Renée Graham

Each December I devote a month's worth of my Sunday column in *The Boston Globe* to memorialize transgender, nonbinary, and gender-nonconforming people who were lost to violence that year. I comb through newspaper articles and GoFundMe pages. I search obituaries, memorial websites, and social media posts. I have watched video recordings of streamed funeral services to listen to eulogies, remembrances, and stories that bring both laughter and sorrow. If only with a few lines, my goal is to convey who these people were before they were taken, how much they loved and were loved, and how deeply they will be missed.

That's how I found Elise Malary's photo.

In a Facebook post, the young woman cradles a vibrant bouquet of sunflowers against her right shoulder. Framed by chestnut brown hair, her delicate features hint of a *Mona Lisa* smile. But it's the declaration on Malary's red T-shirt that grabbed my attention and that lives in my mind every day: YOU DESERVE MORE THAN SURVIVAL.

A beloved thirty-one-year-old Chicago-area transgender rights and anti-racism activist, Malary died in March 2022. Her cause of death was drowning, but its manner was undetermined.[1] Like most of the transgender, nonbinary, and gender-nonconforming people killed that year—and every year since the Human Rights Campaign began tracking such deaths in 2013—she was a Black trans woman.

Between 2013 and 2022, at least 270 transgender, nonbinary, and gender-nonconforming people have been killed in the United States and in Puerto Rico. At least half have died since 2019, when the American Medical Association called violence against the trans community "an epidemic."

Those words—*at least*—bear an impossible burden and truth. Because law enforcement, the media, and surviving family members routinely misgender and "deadname" trans people (refer to them by their obsolete birth name), the real death toll is likely higher. We will never fully know how many succumb to violence every year. We cannot say their names if we don't know their names.

The loss is immeasurable. But I have found inspiration from the words on Malary's T-shirt: YOU DESERVE MORE THAN SURVIVAL. It's a memento of her interrupted life but also a mission statement flush with possibilities for the LGBTQ+ community. We deserve laws that protect us. We deserve political representation that recognizes us. And we deserve a democracy that allows both grace and space for all.

In 2020, in the midst of the COVID-19 pandemic that brought unimaginable sickness, despair, and death, millions filled the streets in protest after Minneapolis police murdered George

Floyd. That atrocity was captured on video for more than nine excruciating minutes. So many knew that what happened to Floyd was not an exception but an unspoken rule. Too many people were dying from the police violence enabled by systemic and institutional racism.

Among the protesters were Black trans women whose community had long been disproportionately targeted by police. A few weeks after Floyd's murder, they seized their moment to be seen and heard. When they arranged their own march for Black trans lives in Brooklyn, more than fifteen thousand people participated.[2] Most wore white to emulate the NAACP's Silent Protest Parade in 1917, when ten thousand people in white marched in silence along Fifth Avenue against anti-Black violence. "Let today be the last day you ever doubt Black trans power," trans activist and writer Raquel Willis told the applauding crowd.

Every day that power is being tested and challenged by Republican-led legislatures. Conservative presidential candidates trip over themselves trying to outdo each other with promises to level cruelty against people who want only to love and live openly. We've witnessed the book bans and curriculums expunged of anything that dares acknowledge LGBTQ+ lives. Hundreds of bills—some now written into law—seek to legislate parts of our community out of existence, including children who identify as trans or nonbinary.

It's the antithesis of democracy.

With all that has happened in recent years, I've struggled to recall a more perilous moment to be queer in my lifetime. I don't say that lightly. In the 1980s I was a young lesbian just out enough to frequent New York's girl bars, but still deeply closeted in the company of family and friends. And like many in my generation, I was attending more memorial services than tea dances. The president, Ronald Reagan, would not publicly utter the word

AIDS until his second term in the White House. By that point, thousands of Americans were already dead and dying. Some of them were my friends and co-workers killed by their government's indifference as much as by the virus itself.

But a great crisis provoked monumental action. Groups like Gay Men's Health Crisis, ACT UP, and Queer Nation were born out of the horror. These groups staged massive protests in 1989 that shut down the stock market and interrupted Sunday services at New York's St. Patrick's Cathedral. Demonstrators held "die-ins" and blocked traffic with their bodies. It was both evocative of the dead and a clear message that people would force the world to stop and hear what needed to be said as long as they were still around to say it. Grief and anger served a purpose even beyond saving the lives of friends, lovers, and those not yet stricken. It brought into bold relief that no one could better fight for us than we ourselves could, and helped fuel the push for same-sex marriage in the United States.

Long before ACT UP created "Silence = Death" as its uncompromising slogan, the LGBTQ+ community had recognized that it had never been afforded the luxury of passivity. We've fought for our full citizenship in this nation, with the understanding that acquiescing meant being accomplices in our own erasure. In 1959 the Cooper's Do-nuts Riot began when queer people, tired of harassment by so-called sexual perversion policing, chased Los Angeles cops from the twenty-four-hour diner.

In 1966, when a San Francisco police officer tried to arrest a trans woman in Compton's Cafeteria, she threw a cup of coffee in his face, and another protest for LGBTQ+ liberation ensued. That same year, borrowing a page from the impactful sit-ins of the civil rights movement, members of the Mattachine Society, then one of this nation's oldest gay rights organizations, identified themselves as gay and asked for drinks at a New York bar.

At that time, the state could legally shut down businesses for serving alcohol to those branded as "sexual deviants." When the case went to court, the odious law was reversed.

That was before June 1969, when trans women of color like Marsha P. Johnson and Sylvia Rivera led an uprising at a mob-owned bar in New York's Greenwich Village called the Stonewall Inn. A night that could have been just one more scarred by the usual police raids and harassment instead sparked the modern movement for LGBTQ+ rights.

From generation to generation, the LGBTQ+ community has mustered the strength and resolve to push this nation to fulfill the promises of American democracy. Black queer people, especially trans women, have long recognized that freedom is intersectional, even as they have often been shut out from the progress they helped to effectuate.

This remains true today. Nearly three months after Floyd's murder, *Time* published "The New American Revolution," a project "that examines America's oppressive past—and the potential for an equitable future." Among the contributors was Imara Jones, founder and CEO of TransLash Media, a multimedia platform that creates and curates trans-affirming content and resources. In her essay, "Why Black Trans Women Are Essential to Our Future," Jones wrote: "Trans people, just through our existence, show the power and the resilience of change, and possibility of how we can do things differently. We are creating a future less defined by gender roles, and defined more by what we can create than what we can destroy."[3]

As the 2024 presidential field was still taking shape—the most important election of our lifetimes since the last most important election of our lifetimes and the one before that—I had a long conversation with Jones. We agreed that in the first presidential election since the white supremacist January 6 insurrection, democracy would again be on the ballot. And that democracy can hold only if it is extended to all regardless of race, religion, sexual orientation, or gender identity. "A more inclusive democracy means constructing a democratic system that is new and not trying to hold on to the one they think they had—because the one they think they had got us to this point," Jones told me.

All those calls for a return to normalcy miss the point that "normal" never accommodated everyone. Broken systems cannot be salvaged. They must all be dismantled. "An inclusive democracy means one that lives up fully to its name. It means the enshrinement of voting rights. It means equal declaration of human rights for all people," Jones added. "The Equality Act has to pass, and it means some sort of [Equal Rights Amendment] where we enshrine the rights of women. The problem is that America has always been about the sequencing and the aggregating of rights among certain people at the expense of others. So a new democracy system that's actually inclusive means we abandon that and create an inclusive democracy in the law to embrace that."

I could not agree more with Jones's assessment. As Marian Wright Edelman, founder of the Children's Defense Fund, once said, democracy "is not a spectator sport." Fighting for Black liberation, women's liberation, and queer liberation must be cooperative, not competitive. Equality for the few ultimately means equality for none. What is taken from me today can be lost to you tomorrow. Unless all Americans fully embrace this idea, our democracy, which is already under attack from enemies within its own borders, won't stand a chance.

LGBTQ+ people have always lived in this country. Being queer has meant fashioning spaces where we were never meant to be. Unwelcome as patrons in various businesses, we opened our own. When our birth families rejected us, we found new sources of familial solace and support. We cared for our sick and buried our dead. We have defied social constructs that try to reduce our true selves to a transitory "lifestyle" and resisted laws against our bodies and against who we love. Black LGBTQ+ people are democracy's stress test. And if democracy fails us, it will eventually fail all.

The fight for freedom and democracy has extended from the streets to the halls of power in record numbers. Since 2018, Black LGBTQ+ representation has increased fourfold, with queer Black women leading the way. At all levels of elected government, the number of Black queer women in politics increased from sixteen in 2018 to fifty-seven in 2023.[4] As Annise Parker, the president and chief executive of the LGBTQ+ Victory Institute, points out, "These leaders are not just disrupting the status quo by fighting for real, generational change, they are inspiring more leaders to either come out publicly or answer the call to public service themselves," she said. "While we have a long way to go . . . the momentum of history is on our side."[5]

These leaders are fighting to build an inclusive and multiracial democracy that creates a lasting space for everyone beyond mere survival—as Malary's T-shirt reminds us. We must work together to bring an end to the infernal cycle of violence against LGBTQ+ people. Together we can carry those who did not live to experience the democracy that these new leaders are trying to make whole. We will say the names of those snatched away by violence and ensure that there will be no more names, known or unknown. The debt we owe to the dead is to protect the living, to stop the loss and grief, and to create a nation where every individual can live in their truth, without compromise or fear of violence. I want my community to live and thrive in the democracy that is our birthright. We all deserve more than survival.

ON FAITH AND LOVE

Rev. Dr. Jacqui Lewis

How proud I was when, as a child, I memorized the Black National Anthem, "Lift Every Voice and Sing." With poetry by NAACP leader James Weldon Johnson set to music by his brother John Rosamond Johnson, this stirring ballad was sung for the first time by five hundred school-age children in Jacksonville, Florida, on February 12, 1900, to celebrate President Lincoln's birthday.[1] "Sing a song full of the faith that the dark past has taught us. / Sing a song full of the hope that the present has brought us. / Facing the rising sun of a new day begun, / let us march on 'till victory is won."

I see those children in my mind's eye, children and grandchildren of recently emancipated Black people with strong backs and expansive hearts, singing a song of hope as resistance to the crushing weight of white supremacy that was already at work in their young lives. A song that expressed—in the face of vicious white rage—Black grief, tenacity, resilience, and joy.

Here we are, over a century later, and quite simply, we have not overcome. In our current context, race and ethnicity, caste and colorism, gender and sexuality, socioeconomic status and education, religion and political party have become reasons for us to be divided and conquered by fear, rancor, and violence. We retreat fully into corners of "us" versus "them." Our differences are magnified in the media—be it social, print, or broadcast—and even in the arts. Too many listen for what we want to hear, what affirms our perspectives, even as those words open and salt our wounds. Our anger baited, we retreat, tribalize, and fume. We don't celebrate the powerful beauty of our diversity; we fear and loathe the differences between us. Those differences are plenty, but I agree with psychologist Robert Carter that race is a different difference.

Though our national folklore boasts of melting pot diversity, what I call "whiteness"—white rage, entitlement, and a sense of superiority—is hardwired into our institutions and will not easily be shaken. And those of us who yearn for liberation from this hot mess of a culture can't pretend that anti-Blackness isn't at the core of what ails us. Even though we pretend to separate church and state, our national religion is white Christian nationalism, a toxic cocktail of racist structures stirred with a mixture of manifest destiny and Protestant exceptionalism. White Christian nationalists believe it's God's intention for white people to rule the world. The stealing of Indigenous land, the erasure of Indigenous people, the enslavement of Africans, centuries of oppression directed at Black people, the rise of the Ku Klux Klan, the insurrection on January 6, 2021, policing out of hand—these are all gifts of whiteness.

Who are we trying to be, as a nation? It is an existential question, answered, I believe, by the concept of *ubuntu*. It comes from the Zulu phrase *Umuntu ngumuntu ngabantu*: "A person is a person through other people." Some translate it as, "I am who I am because we are who we are."

In his 1963 text, *Strength to Love*, Rev. Dr. Martin Luther King, Jr., expressed *ubuntu* in this way: "In a real sense all life is inter-related. All men are caught in an inescapable network of mutuality, tied in a single garment of destiny. Whatever affects one directly, affects all indirectly."[2]

For me, *ubuntu* means that when a child is without clean water in Jackson, Mississippi, or Detroit, Michigan, the human family is thirsty. When a senior citizen in Appalachia can't afford her medications, we are all unwell.

Ubuntu is our birthright; we are all from Africa. Most modern scientists no longer question that humans first evolved in various locations across Africa, particularly southern Africa.[3] It is no coincidence that *ubuntu* developed in that same region.

This ancient wisdom, having emerged in the first human communities, sustained South African activist Nelson Mandela while he was in prison, enabling him to see the humanity of his captors. It was *ubuntu* that fueled the movement that ended apartheid and helped Mandela dream of and work toward a society in which he could proclaim, "Thus, shall we live, because we will have created a society which recognizes that all people are born equal, with each entitled in equal measure to life, liberty, prosperity, human rights and good governance."

When I think of *ubuntu*, I think of fierce love, a bold and brave love that involves ferocious courage and rule-breaking kindness that can heal the world.[4] As was true in South Africa, and as was true in the multiethnic, Black-led Southern freedom movement in the United States, *ubuntu* and fierce love can fuel a revolution to help us rise out of the violence and rage plaguing our current reality.

The kind of love I'm describing is not sentimental love but

rather the demanding, heart-transforming, risk-taking, truth-telling love that insists on justice for all people, no matter who they are, how they look, whom they love, or how they make a living.

Fierce love, to paraphrase Dr. James Loder, delights in the unique particularity of the other, without demand, without possessiveness, but with a kind curiosity and a sense of mutuality. It's a transforming love that breaks through tribalism to help humans realize an inextricable and irrevocable connection, and understand that the liberation, livelihood, and thriving of people and planet are tied up together. The kind of fierce love that is *ubuntu* loves the neighbor—even the stranger—in the same way it loves the self, wanting the entire community to have what is needed.

All the world's major religions have teachings about the relationship between the self and the neighbor. Christianity teaches us to do unto others what we want done to ourselves. Islam teaches not to withhold anything from the other that we desire for ourselves. Hindus learn to do nothing to another that they would not want done to them. Judaism teaches to love the neighbor as the self and, even more stridently, to love the stranger, because Jewish people were once strangers in a strange land. Our Sikh siblings are taught to do nothing to break another's heart.

In the United States, out of a population of 330 million people, 186 million identify as religious, the majority practicing Christianity, Judaism, Islam, Hinduism, and the Sikh faith.[5] Imagine what our culture would be like if the neighbor-love demanded by our faith guided our ethical commitments. Imagine the policies that would be generated if our elected officials who claim faith shared resources with the neighbor as with the self. Imagine the politics, the discourse in the public square, if we were guided by "Love your neighbor as you love yourself" or "Don't do anything to break anyone else's heart."

What if the way we embraced racial and ethnic diversity were guided by *ubuntu*—"I am who I am because you are who you are. I can't be who I am unless you are fully yourself." What if we fully embraced the fact that our surviving and thriving were interconnected? What if we, in our diverse faith perspectives, tried to love the stranger? What if—beyond faith—we embraced the science that we are all from Africa? That there is only one race, and that's humanity, and that pseudo-race science caused the terrible lie that some of us are less than the others? How would that change the way race matters in America?

Ubuntu and fierce love foster the empathy needed to understand that how we vote, where we live, how we shop, and what kind of media we consume are all choices that impact the human family. *Ubuntu* and fierce love would have thwarted the stealing of land from Indigenous people because the settlers who came to Turtle Island would have acknowledged the humanity of the people living here. *Ubuntu* and fierce love would have made chattel slavery impossible because humans would not have been able to bind the ankles and wrists of other humans, pack them like sardines in ships, strip them of dignity and rights, and treat them as if they were three-fifths human.

Because that happened, because humans were sold and chained and disenfranchised, *ubuntu* and fierce love call for truth, reconciliation, and reparations paid to the millions in the African diaspora who were crippled by this evil institution. As Ta-Nehisi Coates wrote in *The Atlantic*, "Two hundred fifty years of slavery. Ninety years of Jim Crow. Sixty years of separate but equal. Thirty-five years of racist housing policy. Until we reckon with our compounding moral debts, America will never be whole."[6]

We can be reparations people. We can repair what white supremacist ideologies have done to us all. Reparations start with you and me. Every human being in this nation and on the planet can begin to repair the harm done not only to Black people but to the human family by white supremacist ideologies. Because we are all one, white supremacy wounds and weakens all of us. As we seek to be an anti-racist society, build an inclusive democracy, and repair the deep brokenness that whiteness caused in our shared living, fierce love requires us to take several steps.

First, we must acknowledge that this nation's systems and structures were built with the assumption of white supremacy as a base. That truth needs to be acknowledged, interrogated, and used as a guide to reform how those systems—education, health care, law, prisons, policing, housing, even the arts—work. They are broken and must be repaired. But first we must tell the truth on them; the truth will set us free.

Second, we must recognize that each of us has power in a sphere of influence to be an agent of change in the way the system works. What we say, write, speak; what we read, share, introject into our psyches; how we raise our children, engage with our neighbors and families—all these are opportunities to do better. We can and we must.

Third, we must understand, to paraphrase Mandela, that love must be taught. We must teach one another to love. Period. For some folks, talk about love sounds weak, but from my point of view, love is the strongest force on the planet.

And fourth, we must raise generations of children who are taught the truth, who are encouraged to create safe and brave spaces for truth-telling, so there can be repair and racial reconciliation. The children are listening and watching and learning from what we do and what we don't do. We must not protect them by lying to them about our past; we must guide them to a healed world and a working democracy. We must teach them fierce love—not denial, not power-over, not fearful existence in silos and tribes. *Ubuntu*. Fierce love.

The kind of love that is fierce—that is *ubuntu*—crosses borders and boundaries. It makes new cultural rules. It cares for the stranger. It turns strangers into friends. Fierce love makes us change the channel on the television, change the dial on the radio, and change our minds about messages about the other and discover how much humanity we have in common. It increases our communities.

This became clear to me many years ago. As a young woman, I survived a car accident in Windsor, Ontario. Alone, with no money and a totaled car, I encountered a Canadian woman, a stranger, who held me while I wept, bought me food, checked me into a hotel, paid my way, and picked me up the next morning to help me get back to my hometown. She was white, I am Black. She was Canadian, I am American. She didn't know me, but she saw our human connection and helped me. She loved me fiercely—with *ubuntu* love.

Ubuntu is our heritage. It's in our human story. It's our birthright. With *ubuntu*, we can learn to see the world not only through our own stories—through our own eyes—but also through the stories and worldview of the stranger, the one least like us. *Ubuntu* is a superpower available to all of us. It can fuel our movement against American apartheid, against the violence rooted in white supremacy. *Ubuntu* can help us win the ideological battle our hearts and minds are waging for freedom from hatred and bigotry. With *ubuntu*, we can march on until victory is won.

ON VIOLENCE AGAINST BLACK WOMEN

Hon. Ruth Richardson

The most disrespected person in America is the Black woman. The most unprotected person in America is the Black woman. The most neglected person in America is the Black woman.

—Malcolm X

I am the first Black woman elected from my district to serve in the Minnesota House of Representatives. In 2019, during my first term in a body of 134 members, there were only three Black women. I have always regarded myself as an accidental politician because I had no long-term plan or strategy to seek elected office. I was also unaware, when I began running in my district, that I would make history as a first. The campaign journey was intense, and I felt the unrelenting stings of thousands of micro- and macroaggressions, including the words of critics telling me I was not qualified for the job or demanding that I wait my turn. On election night, as the results came in, I realized that I had made history. Flipping a red seat by eight points, I was headed to the capitol.

Carrying the banner of "the first" was a heavy weight, and I knew I could not waste a moment of this opportunity. A descendant of enslaved peoples, the great-granddaughter of a midwife, the granddaughter of sharecroppers, and the daughter of parents who grew up picking cotton in the fields of Mississippi and Alabama, I know the sorrow of struggle and injustice. I now had the power of policy in my grasp. By the end of my first two-year term in office, eighteen bills that I had chief authored were signed into law, but the bills advocating for Black women, which were the greatest priorities for me, had gained no traction.

Despite my efforts, I was unable to get a hearing on my bill to establish the nation's first task force on Missing and Murdered Black Women and Girls or on my Dignity in Pregnancy and Childbirth bill, to address the current Black maternal health crisis. In the final minutes of the session on the house floor—with full knowledge that my highest-priority bills would likely not succeed—I reflected on the enduring legacy of ignoring Black women in the United States.

Despite this painful reality, Black women have made extraordinary contributions to the success, wealth, and prosperity of this nation. For centuries we have served as the backbone of communities as healers, prayer partners, organizers, caregivers, workers, freedom fighters, storytellers, keepers of tradition, and unwavering defenders of justice. We are American history.

Yet beginning with the brutally violent exploitation of the slave trade, Black women have been disrespected, unprotected, and neglected. Violence against Black women was institutionalized in the founding of this nation, and that harmful traumatic legacy of violence continues today.[1] Black women in the United States experience among the highest rates of physical violence, sexual violence, human trafficking, incarceration, homicide, maternal mortality, and family separation through child welfare policing policies. And Black girls are consistently pushed out of the nation's schools, fueling the school-to-prison pipeline and contributing to poverty.

The data are disturbing, unacceptable, and embarrassing for a wealthy nation. The outcomes we see today are not surprises but rather predictable outcomes of a system that is working the way it was designed to work. Research has proved that deep disparities exist for Black women, and a move from data to solutions is long overdue. Behind those numbers are real people and families with hopes, dreams, and purpose bearing trauma, pain, and loss. Black women's voices and experiences are essential for understanding and addressing this crisis of violence. In fact, Black women have long played the roles of truth teller, conscience of the nation, defender of democracy, and have been offering strategies and solutions for building a more just nation for centuries as we navigated the deadly consequences of systemic racism.

In 2020, as I drafted Minnesota House Resolution number 1, "Declaring Racism a Public Health Crisis," I reflected on the legacy of Dr. Rebecca Lee Crumpler, the first Black woman physician in the United States, who received her degree at the end of the Civil War. She authored a book on infant and maternal health that emphasized the "possibilities of prevention"— ways to prevent diseases and ailments—rather than treatment and cure.[2] Because of racism and sexism, Crumpler's peers disregarded her work. She experienced trouble getting prescriptions filled, she was not allowed admitting privileges at local hospitals, and she endured ridicule from administrators and doctors who ignored her presence or cruelly suggested that the "M.D." behind her name stood for Mule Driver. For over 125 years, the works and contributions of the first Black woman physician were ignored. Only recently have her work and scholarship been acknowledged. And it begs the question: how much further could we be as a nation if Dr. Crumpler's work had not been dismissed?

While I faced the risk of my own efforts being dismissed in the Minnesota House of Representatives, I decided to forge ahead with a resolution to acknowledge the deadly impact of systemic racism in the United States. The Minnesota House became the first chamber in the nation to declare racism a public health crisis and created the House Select Committee on Racial Justice. Following our lead, seven other state chambers declared racism a public health crisis. The House Select Committee on Racial Justice began a long-overdue conversation in the Minnesota legislature in conjunction with members of the community. We published a report containing eighty-three community-driven recommendations, centering the voices of those closest to the pain.

The work of the House Select Committee on Racial Justice set the foundation for Minnesota to become the first state in the nation to create a task force on Missing and Murdered Black Women and Girls. I was inspired by the work of former Minnesota representative Mary Kunesh, who was instrumental in creating the nation's first Missing and Murdered Indigenous Relatives task force. She was my sister in justice, championing passage of the bill in the Minnesota Senate and serving with me on the task force. I was also moved by the relentless advocacy of sisters-in-law Derrica and Natalie Wilson, co-founders of the Black and Missing Foundation. Derrica's story was powerful as she joined the Falls Church City Police Department in 2002 as the first Black female officer in the department's history. In her role as an officer, she had seen the stark disparities in law enforcement resources and media coverage of missing Black women and girls. She realized that cases involving Black women and girls stayed open four times longer than those of their white peers.

In the HBO documentary *Black and Missing*, she recounts

investigating a case that had originated with a domestic violence call. When she encountered the two people involved, she was able to ascertain that the young Black woman who been beaten had been abducted. The young woman's hair had been pulled out of her scalp, and she had bite marks all over her body. They sent her to the hospital to get a rape kit. For days her abductor had held her captive in a motel in Falls Church. She had been reported missing in a neighboring jurisdiction, yet the flyer never crossed Derrica's desk. It was this impact of seeing Black women and girls' cases ignored that motivated Derrica to help establish the Black and Missing Foundation.

We cannot stay silent about the violence against Black women in the United States. It is a pervasive problem that undermines American democracy. If we hope to build the kind of society that regards all people as equal and significant, we must devise strategies to protect those who are marginalized. The protection of Black women is therefore an essential part of any vision of an inclusive democracy. This is an uphill battle, but there are steps we can take. We must reject the harmful narrative of color-blind approaches and strategies that shield—rather than confront—the racial disparities in this country. We must educate ourselves and our children on the history of our people in the United States. And we must work together to protect Black women. This nation's crisis of inequality was not created by Black people, and it cannot be solved by Black people alone. We must forge alliances, despite our many differences, to devise community-based responses and solutions to the crisis facing Black women.

As a nation, we are at crossroads. Violence against Black women and girls is an urgent public health crisis. We require better coordination at the state and federal level to protect Black women and girls. Federally, we need dedicated and ongoing support, resources, and funding streams to address domestic and intimate partner violence, housing insecurity, and wage disparities. We must also work to strengthen our school systems for all students and focus on eliminating school discipline disparities. We need culturally intelligent educators and administrators who are committed to anti-racism. We also need investments in our youth and in places where they see reflections of themselves.

For centuries, Black women and girls have been unprotected and vulnerable, and they still are. It is therefore critical that we build an infrastructure of places and task forces where Black women and girls can find shelter and safety. We must dedicate financial and human resources to address this epidemic of violence. One-time funding and temporary grants are not sufficient to protect Black women and girls. It is also imperative that we work collaboratively to disrupt systems of oppression and reject the narrative that they are the norm. Accepting the status quo means that we continue to live with rampant and disproportionate violence against Black women and girls.

Minnesota has now provided a powerful blueprint for the next steps forward. The Missing and Murdered Black Women and Girls (MMBWG) task force in the state should be extended to the nation. We ultimately need a national and permanent MMBWG office that improves data collection on violence against Black women and girls, traces the root causes of such violence, and dedicates resources to its prevention. A national office would provide infrastructure to offer supportive services to survivors and families, work to reform our Amber Alert and missing-person-alert systems, eliminate the harmful classification of "runaway," and prioritize resources and collaboration to help solve cold cases. To build a democracy that meets the needs of all citizens, we must commit to addressing domestic violence, intimate partner violence, human trafficking, sexual and labor exploitation, gang violence, the adultification and sexualization of Black girls, disparities in our foster care system, and homelessness.[3] Protecting Black women and girls also means confronting systemic racism, poverty, the lack of mental health services, police brutality, substance use disorders, and even the media's perpetuation of stereotypical images.

Our collective voices are powerful as we fight for this nation to live up to the promise that all are created equal and endowed with the rights of life, liberty, and pursuit of happiness. To hold the United States to this promise, Black women must have a seat at the table where decisions are made. It is therefore critical that we elect Black women to office and strengthen our collective political power. Black women have been through so much, and our experiences, voices, and stories matter. When Black women and girls are thriving, all other Americans will benefit.

For centuries Black women have shown up, spoken up, and fought to build a nation that is better than the one we have today. There is an enduring legacy of our work to build an inclusive democracy where everyone truly can thrive—grounded in justice, protection, and equity.

ON RACISM AND FATPHOBIA

Tami Sawyer

The slogan "Trust Black Women" now circulates throughout social media and in mainstream news. Popularized in
reproductive justice spaces, the phrase has become a ral-
lying cry among liberal activists.[1] It has gained traction in recent
years as Black women continue to leave their mark on American
politics. Hearkening back to the heroic efforts of pioneers such as
Fannie Lou Hamer, the civil rights activist; Shirley Chisolm, the
first Black woman to be elected to the U.S. Congress; and Angela
Davis, the Black Power activist, "Trust Black Women" calls on
Americans to alter their thinking and incorporate Black women
into their vision of a successful democracy. I believe this is necessary if we truly desire to build an inclusive democracy. Even
within the spaces that appear most progressive, Black women
must be empowered and supported and, more important, have

access to real power. This means *all* Black women—including those who are often disparaged by others and pushed to the sidelines on account of their weight and appearance.

According to the U.S. Department of Health and Human Services, 80 percent of adult Black women are considered medically obese.[2] By this estimate, most Black women in the United States do not meet the white standard of beauty: small and slender. When Black women fail to meet this standard, we experience disrespect and are disempowered.

I learned this difficult lesson while I was serving in public office. A few days after November 3, 2020, a retired white man posted a photo of an elected official in Memphis, Tennessee. He was commenting on the results of the 2020 presidential election, a conversation that clogged public discourse in the United States for weeks. Below the photo of this elected official, he wrote, "I believe I hear her beginning to sing. I don't like her singing but it certainly sounds like the FAT LADY."[3] He was referring to me.

My experiences are not unique. Other Black women who do not fit white beauty standards endure the same attacks from those who wish to diminish their power and influence because of their race, gender, and size. This troubling pattern must come to an end if this nation intends to live up to ideals. An inclusive democracy is not possible when some Americans are treated with disdain simply for not fitting into some man-made mold of what the "ideal" woman is supposed to look like.

The challenges that curvy Black women face in political leadership stem from a longer history of racism, sexism, and fatphobia in the United States and throughout the African diaspora. The transatlantic slave trade placed Black women into forced servitude in the homes and communities of white Europeans and Americans, forcing them to make space for Black women's bodies. Sociologist Sabrina Strings argues that, in order to make a distinction between white women and Black women, "the body has been used to craft and legitimate race, sex, and class hierarchies." Western institutions of religion, health, and media have become complicit in developing a "fear of the imagined 'fat black woman.'" According to Strings, "This was created by racial and religious ideologies that have been used to both degrade black women and discipline white women."[4]

In the early nineteenth century, Sarah Baartman (known as the "Hottentot Venus"), an African woman who was enslaved, spent much of her short life being trafficked across Europe as a sideshow for white Europeans. Because of the ample size of her body, chest, and buttocks, Baartman was studied, prodded, and sexually assaulted. When she died in 1815 around the age of twenty-six, her remains were preserved and displayed in museums. The denigration of Black women and their bodies in European and American history ultimately set the stage for modern anti-Black fatphobia in public discourse.[5]

In 1961, Ancel Keys, the founder of the Body Mass Index (BMI), spoke to *Time* magazine about his research on obesity. Though unrelated to his findings, Keys chose to describe obesity as offensive and expressed his disgust for Americans who did not fit white beauty standards. Mainstream women's magazines, such as *Cosmopolitan* and *Harper's Bazaar*, reinforced this point of view.[6] Slimness became a marker of class that was reserved for white women. Black women were considered gluttonous and lazy, lacking intelligence, purity, and grace.

These ideas seeped into the civil rights movement. In 1964, Fannie Lou Hamer, a curvy Black woman, encountered disdain from others who were far more interested in her looks than in her ideas. Even after delivering a powerful speech before the Democratic National Convention, Hamer's "visual image," including her dress and vernacular style, were constant points of reference in the media and, at times, among her associates.[7] Instead of recognizing the power of Hamer's testimony and experiences, Roy Wilkins, then executive secretary of the NAACP, criticized Hamer's clothing and reportedly asked someone to "do something about her dress." Another activist later remarked that Hamer "wore old tattered clothes and she was not physically attractive."[8] The degradation Hamer endured on account of her appearance did not stop the activist from making her place in history. Yet her experiences illuminate the persistence of racism and fatphobia in American society.

Black feminist scholar Brittney Cooper's recent experiences are another example of how Black women with curves continue to be treated with disrespect in American society. A week before the presidential election of November 2020, Cooper argued on Twitter that Black women should withhold sex from Black men as a way to influence them to vote against Donald Trump.[9] Her recommendation was made in jest—she was playing off the storylines in the Greek play *Lysistrata* by Aristophanes and in its modern retelling in Spike Lee's *Chi-Raq*. Yet almost immediately Black men and white supporters of Donald Trump began to attack Cooper for her tweet by focusing on her weight. Their response revealed their disdain that a fat Black woman such as Cooper would be considered desirable for sexual intercourse or have the choice to withhold sex from a partner. In the face of these verbal attacks on her body image and aspersions about her desirability, Cooper enacted agency by owning her identity as a fat Black woman in a positive way. She then affirmed her desirability and the respect owed to her while offering proof of supportive and loving relationships with Black men in her life.

Watching these events unfold online took me back to the moment I campaigned to be the first woman mayor of Memphis, Tennessee. It was 2019, and I was busy doing interviews, sharing with the residents of Memphis my ideas about how I would improve conditions in the city. During this time, my body was on display twenty-four hours a day, and to my surprise, my weight was constantly the subject of conversation in the media. In August 2019, *Memphis* magazine released its September issue. The cover was inscribed with the title "The Race for Memphis." Below were three caricatures of the leading candidates: two older men—one white and one Black—and me. While caricatures are meant to exaggerate the features of the illustrated subject, the image of me was shocking. The artist, Chris Ellis, who is white, chose to present my image in a grotesque manner. His image shifted past a caricature to that of a minstrel cartoon. When I confronted him about the drawing, he stood his ground and defended his work. In a subsequent Facebook post, he went further to suggest that I deserved the illustration and described me as a "monstrously obese woman of color."[10]

My campaign manager and I chose to make space for others to address the hurtful depiction. The cover sparked outrage locally and nationally, including admonitions from NAACP leaders Derrick Johnson and Cornell Brooks. Conversely, some challenged the outrage and accused my campaign of playing the proverbial race card for sympathy.[11] Yet the broad community response, or what I call the "mass clapback," was an empowering moment for me. When we resist efforts to disparage overweight Black women, we send a powerful message about what a democracy should look like. Fat Black women have a place in leadership as much as anyone else in the United States, and our perspectives matter.

My exchange with Maya Rupert, then the campaign manager for presidential candidate Julián Castro, reaffirmed my position. When the grotesque illustration of me went viral, Rupert sent me a direct message on Twitter to encourage and affirm me. As a Black woman in the public eye, she had experienced her share of fatphobia and *misogynoir*—a term introduced by scholar Moya Bailey that refers to the misogyny directed specifically at Black women.[12] By reaching out, Rupert reminded me that my experience was not isolated and, more important, that other Black women had my back.

My experiences in public office have not been easy, but they have taught me a lot about democracy. At its core, a democracy should allow space for all citizens to participate in the political process. Yet what I have witnessed in the United States is a pattern of exclusion when it comes to Black women—especially Black women who do not fit white standards of what weight is perceived as ideal or acceptable. Despite our diverse talents and contributions, Black women in politics are often undermined by the powerful. We are disparaged for our looks—viewed as not pretty enough or skinny enough to be taken seriously. In a real democracy, *all* Black women, including the curvy ones, would have an opportunity to serve and lead without constant disrespect.

The democracy that I envision is inclusive of everyone—including me. The voices of Black women—regardless of class, education, and size—are powerful. As author Tressie McMillan Cottom argues, we must "adjust [our] assumptions about who does and does not belong in the body politic."[13] It would behoove all Americans to take Black women seriously and extend to us the respect and trust we deserve.

ACKNOWLEDGMENTS

I'm thankful to God for helping me finish this project. The support I received along the way is a testament to his grace and favor.

This book would not have been possible without the kindness of so many wonderful people. I'm grateful to the twenty-two brilliant Black women who agreed to contribute essays. Editing can be a challenging exercise, but it's especially rewarding to work with a group of talented, passionate, and sharp writers and thinkers. I'll forever cherish the opportunity I had to collaborate with them.

Heartfelt thanks to my amazing editor, Amy Cherry, who enthusiastically supported my idea for this project from day one and worked closely with me over the last year to help me complete it. Her support, as well as the support of her colleagues at

ACKNOWLEDGMENTS

W. W. Norton, including Huneeya Siddiqui, has been invaluable. The same is true for my literary agent, Don Fehr, who quickly embraced my idea for this project and diligently worked to secure the perfect home for it.

Advice and assistance from a community of friends, near and far, made all the difference as I worked to transform an idea into reality. Two excellent research assistants—Richard Mares and Mickell Carter—helped to lighten the load as I worked through various tasks.

I'm so grateful to my family for their unwavering support—especially my husband, Jay, who cheered me on to the finish line. This book will forever hold a special place in our hearts—we welcomed our second child just as I was putting the final touches on the volume.

Last but certainly not least, thank you to each of you who picked up this book and decided to explore its contents. I hope the essays leave a lasting, positive impression on you. And above all, I hope they offer guidance for steps you might take to help make this nation—and world—better.

CONTRIBUTOR BIOGRAPHIES

Aimee Allison is the founder and president of She the People, a national organization that elevates the voice and power of women of color as leaders of a new multiracial political and cultural era.

Keisha N. Blain is professor of Africana Studies and History at Brown University. She is a columnist for MSNBC, a Guggenheim Fellow, and author, most recently, of the National Book Critics Circle Award finalist *Until I Am Free*.

Rhea Boyd, M.D., M.P.H., is a pediatrician, public health advocate, and scholar who writes and teaches on structural racism, inequity, and health.

Hon. Carol Moseley Braun is a former U.S. senator, diplomat, politician, and lawyer. She was the first African American woman to serve in the U.S. Senate and the first female senator from Illinois.

Donna Brazile is a veteran Democratic political strategist, author, ABC News contributor, columnist for *The Grio*, and former interim chair of the Democratic National Committee. She is also an adjunct professor of Women and Gender Studies at Georgetown University.

Hon. Laphonza Butler is a senator from California and the president of EMILYs List, the nation's largest resource for women in politics. She leads its efforts to elect Democratic pro-choice women across the country, up and down the ballot.

Taifa Smith Butler is the president of Demos, a national think tank that champions solutions to create a democracy and economy rooted in racial equity. She previously led the Georgia Budget and Policy Institute.

Glynda C. Carr is the president and CEO of Higher Heights Leadership Fund and Higher Heights for America, the only national organization exclusively dedicated to expanding Black women's elected representation.

Charlene A. Carruthers is a writer, filmmaker, and social justice leader. As the founding national director of BYP100 (Black Youth Project 100), she worked alongside hundreds of young Black activists to build a member-led organization dedicated to creating justice and freedom for all Black people.

Alicia Garza is the co-founder of #BlackLivesMatter and the Black Lives Matter Global Network, an international organizing project to end state violence against and oppression of Black people.

Renée Graham is an award-winning opinion columnist and associate editor for *The Boston Globe*. She writes on race and racism, domestic violence, LGBTQ+ issues, police misconduct, gun control, and politics.

Hon. Crystal Hudson is the council member for New York City's District 35 in Brooklyn, representing the neighborhoods of Prospect Heights, Fort Greene, Clinton Hill, and parts of Crown Heights and Bedford-Stuyvesant. She was elected in 2021 and made history as one of the first out gay Black women ever elected in New York City.

Hon. Sheila Jackson Lee is an influential and forceful voice in Washington. She has served as a member of the U.S. House of Representatives since 1995. She represents the 18th Congressional District of Texas, which includes most of central Houston.

Hon. Kim Michelle Janey served as Boston's first woman and first Black mayor in 2021, successfully leading the city through a multitude of unprecedented challenges, including the COVID-19 global pandemic. She is currently the president and CEO of Economic Mobility Pathways (EMPath).

Mariame Kaba is one of the nation's leading abolitionists and an organizer and educator who is active in movements for racial, gender, and transformative justice. She is the founder and director of Project NIA, a grassroots organization with a vision to end youth incarceration, and the co-founder of Interrupting Criminalization.

Andraéa LaVant is a nationally and internationally sought-after disability inclusion expert. She is widely recognized for spearheading a global disability justice movement as impact producer for Netflix's Oscar-nominated film *Crip Camp*. She is founder and president of LaVant Consulting, Inc.

Rev. Dr. Jacqui Lewis is the senior minister at Middle Church. She uses her gifts as author, activist, preacher, and public theologian to creating an anti-racist, just, gun-violence-free, fully welcoming, gender-affirming society in which everyone has enough.

Atima Omara, past president of Young Democrats of America, is an award-winning political strategist. She is the founder and CEO of Omara Strategy Group, which provides consultation to progressive candidates and organizations to help them win campaigns.

Hon. Ruth Richardson is an American politician and member of the Minnesota House of Representatives. In 2022 she authored a bill that passed the Minnesota House to establish the nation's first dedicated office for Missing and Murdered Black Women and Girls.

Tami Sawyer is an American politician and activist. From 2018 to 2022, she served as a Shelby County commissioner and the Black Caucus chair in her hometown of Memphis, Tennessee.

Vilissa Thompson, L.M.S.W., is a disability rights consultant, writer, and activist. She is the founder and CEO of Ramp Your Voice!, an organization focused on promoting self-advocacy and empowerment among disabled people.

Hon. Nina Turner served as an Ohio State Senator and national co-chair for the Bernie Sanders 2020 presidential campaign. She is currently a senior fellow at the New School's Institute on Race, Power and Political Economy and host of *UnBossed* on TYT Network.

Raquel Willis is an award-winning writer and activist dedicated to Black transgender liberation. She has held groundbreaking posts throughout her career, including director of communications for the Ms. Foundation for Women, executive editor of *Out* magazine, and national organizer for the Transgender Law Center.

NOTES

INTRODUCTION

1. For a broad overview of Fannie Lou Hamer's life and ideas, see Keisha N. Blain, *Until I Am Free: Fannie Lou Hamer's Enduring Message to America* (Boston: Beacon Press, 2021).
2. Fannie Lou Hamer, " 'What Have We to Hail?,' Speech Delivered in Kentucky, Summer 1968," in *The Speeches of Fannie Lou Hamer: To Tell It Like It Is*, eds. Maegan Parker Brooks and Davis W. Houck (Jackson: University Press of Mississippi, 2011), 82.
3. *Shelby County v. Holder*, 570 U.S. 529 (2013).
4. Karine Jean-Pierre, "2009–2014: The Shelby Ruling," in *Four Hundred Souls: A Community History of African America, 1619–2019*, eds. Ibram X. Kendi and Keisha N. Blain (New York: One World, 2021): 378–81; "The Effects of Shelby County v. Holder," Brennan Center for Justice, August 6, 2018, https://www.brennancenter.org/our-work/policy-solutions/effects-shelby -county-v-holder.
5. Kristin McIntosh et al., "Examining the Black-white Wealth Gap," Brookings Institution, February 27, 2020, https://www.brookings.edu/blog/up -front/2020/02/27/examining-the-black-white-wealth-gap/.
6. Moritz Kuhn, Moritz Schularick, and Ulrike I. Steins, "Income and Wealth

Inequality in America, 1949–2016," *Journal of Political Economy* 128, no. 9 (September 2020): 1, https://www.minneapolisfed.org/research/institute -working-papers/income-and-wealth-inequality-in-america-1949-2016.

7. McIntosh et al., "Examining the Black-white Wealth Gap."

8. Frank Edwards, Hedwig Lee, and Michael Esposito, "Risk of Being Killed by Police Use of Force in the United States by Age, Race-Ethnicity, and Sex," *PNAS* 116, no. 34 (August 2019): 16793–98, https://www.pnas.org/doi/ full/10.1073/pnas.1821204116.

9. Kimberlé Williams Crenshaw and Andrea J. Ritchie, *Say Her Name: Resisting Police Brutality Against Black Women* (New York: African American Policy Forum and Columbia Law School's Center for Intersectionality and Social Policy Studies, July 2015), https://www.aapf.org/_files/ugd/62e126_8752f05 75a22470ba7c7be7f723ed6ee.pdf.

10. Latoya Hill, Samantha Artiga, and Usha Ranji, "Racial Disparities in Maternal and Infant Health: Current Status and Efforts to Address Them," KFF, November 1, 2022, https://www.kff.org/racial-equity-and-health-policy/issue -brief/racial-disparities-in-maternal-and-infant-health-current-status-and -efforts-to-address-them/; Latoya Hill and Samantha Artiga, "COVID-19 Cases and Deaths by Race/Ethnicity: Current Data and Changes Over Time," KFF, August 22, 2022, https://www.kff.org/coronavirus-covid-19/issue-brief/ covid-19-cases-and-deaths-by-race-ethnicity-current-data-and-changes-over -time/.

11. Linda Darling-Hammond, "Unequal Opportunity: Race and Education," Brookings Institution, March 1, 1998, https://www.brookings.edu/articles/ unequal-opportunity-race-and-education/; Emma Garcia, "Schools Are Still Segregated and Black Children Are Paying the Price," Economy Policy Institute, February 12, 2020, https://www.epi.org/publication/schools-are-still -segregated-and-black-children-are-paying-a-price/.

12. Patricia Mazzei and Anemona Hartocollis, "Florida Rejects A.P. African American Studies Class," *New York Times*, January 19, 2023.

13. Morgan Matzen, "House passes Gov. Kristi Noem's Bills Aiming to Ban Critical Race Theory, Divisive Concepts," *Argus Leader*, February 15, 2022, https://www.argusleader.com/story/news/education/2022/02/15/critical-race -theory-crt-bills-kristi-noem-passed-south-dakota/6803497001/.

14. See Claudia Jones, *An End to the Neglect of the Problems of the Negro Woman!* (New York: National Women's Commission of the CPUSA, 1949); Keeanga-Yamahtta Taylor, ed., *How We Get Free: Black Feminism and the Combahee River Collective* (Chicago: Haymarket Books, 2017).

15. Maya Harris, "Women of Color: A Growing Force in the American Electorate," Center for American Progress, October 30, 2014, https://www .americanprogress.org/article/women-of-color/.

16. "Black Girl Magic: The Power of Black Women in Elections," AFL-CIO, September 27, 2016, https://aflcio.org/sites/default/files/2017-03/AFL -CIO%2BBlack%2BWomen%2BVote.pdf.

17. Matt Stiles, "Census: Black Voting Rate Topped Rate for Whites In 2012," NPR, May 8, 2013.

18. Jens Manuel Krogstad and Mark Hugo Lopez, "Black Voter Turnout Fell in 2016, Even as a Record Number of Americans Cast Ballots," Pew Research Center, May 12, 2017, https://www.pewresearch.org/fact-tank/2017/05/12/black-voter-turnout-fell-in-2016-even-as-a-record-number-of-americans-cast-ballots/.

19. Center for American Women and Politics, "Gender Differences in Voter Turnout," Rutgers Eagleton Institute of Politics, https://cawp.rutgers.edu/facts/voters/gender-differences-voter-turnout#GGN.

20. Rachael Davis, "Polling Results Estimate 94 Percent of Black Women Voters Chose Hillary Clinton," *Essence*, October 26, 2020.

21. Martha S. Jones, "1774–1779: The American Revolution," in *Four Hundred Souls: A Community History of African America, 1619–2019*, eds. Ibram X. Kendi and Keisha N. Blain (New York: One World, 2021), 139–42.

22. Darlene Superville, "Biden Signs Bill Making Lynching a Federal Hate Crime," Associated Press, March 29, 2022. On Wells-Barnett, see Mia Bay, *To Tell The Truth Freely: The Life of Ida B. Wells* (New York: Hill and Wang, 2009); Paula Giddings, *Ida: A Sword Among Lions: Ida B. Wells and the Campaign Against Lynching* (New York: HarperCollins, 2008); Patricia Schechter, *Ida B. Wells-Barnett and American Reform, 1880–1930* (Chapel Hill: University of North Carolina Press, 2001).

23. See Erik S. McDuffie, *Sojourning for Freedom: Black Women, American Communism, and the Making of Black Left Feminism* (Durham, N.C.: Duke University Press, 2011); Dayo Gore, *Radicalism at the Crossroads: African American Women Activists in the Cold War* (New York: New York University Press, 2011); and Keisha N. Blain, *Set the World on Fire: Black Nationalist Women and the Global Struggle for Freedom* (Philadelphia: University of Pennsylvania Press, 2018).

ON WOMEN'S RIGHTS

1. Kimberlé Crenshaw, "Demarginalizing the Intersection of Race and Sex: A Black Feminist Critique of Antidiscrimination Doctrine, Feminist Theory and Antiracist Politics," *University of Chicago Legal Forum* 1989, no. 1 (1989): 139–67.

2. Abigail Adams to John Adams, March 31, 1776, *Adams Family Papers: An Electronic Archive*, Massachusetts Historical Society, http://www.masshist.org/digitaladams.

3. Abigail Adams to John Adams, September 22, 1774, Adams Family Papers, http://www.masshist.org/digitaladams.

4. See Edith B. Gelles, *Abigail Adams: A Writing Life* (New York: Routledge, 2002), and Woody Holton, *Abigail Adams: A Life* (New York: Free Press, 2009).

5. Moya Bailey, *Misogynoir Transformed: Black Women's Digital Resistance* (New York: New York University Press, 2021).

ON REPRODUCTIVE FREEDOM

1. Keisha N. Blain, *Until I Am Free: Fannie Lou Hamer's Enduring Message to America* (Boston: Beacon Press, 2021), 39.

2. Isabelle Taft, "Mississippi Remains Deadliest State for Babies, CDC Data Shows," *Mississippi Today*, September 29, 2022, https://mississippitoday .org/2022/09/29/mississippi-remains-deadliest-state-for-babies/.

3. Taft, "Mississippi Remains Deadliest State for Babies"; U.S. National Library of Medicine, *Postpartum Medicaid: Addressing Gaps in Coverage to Improve Maternal Health* (Jackson: Center for Mississippi Health Policy, February 2021), http://resource.nlm.nih.gov/101778858.

4. Nandita Bose, "Roe v. Wade Ruling Disproportionately Hurts Black Women, Experts Say," Reuters, June 27, 2022.

5. Katherine Gallagher Robbins and Shaina Goodman, "State Abortion Bans Could Harm Nearly 15 Million Women of Color," National Partnership for Women and Families, July 2022, https://www.nationalpartnership.org/our -work/health/reports/state-abortion-bans-harm-woc.html.

6. Katy Backes Kozhimannil, Asha Hassan, and Rachel R. Hardeman, "Abortion Access as a Racial Justice Issue," *New England Journal of Medicine* 387 (October 27, 2022): 1537–39, https://www.nejm.org/doi/full/10.1056/ NEJMp2209737.

7. Bose, "Roe v. Wade Ruling."

8. Liza Fuentes, "Inequity in U.S. Abortion Rights and Access: The End of Roe Is Deepening Existing Divides," Guttmacher Institute, January 17, 2023, https://www.guttmacher.org/2023/01/inequity-us-abortion-rights-and-access -end-roe-deepening-existing-divides.

9. Eugene Daniels and Myah Ward, "Harris on GOP's Anti-Abortion Push: 'How Dare They,'" *Politico*, May 3, 2022, https://www.politico.com/ news/2022/05/03/kamala-harris-supreme-court-abortion-00029813.

10. Coretta Scott King. *My Life with Martin Luther King, Jr.* (New York: Henry Holt, 1993).

11. Marcia Gillespie, "African American Women Are for Reproductive Freedom—We Remember," Berkeley Law, 1989, https://www.law.berkeley.edu/ php-programs/centers/crrj/zotero/loadfile.php?entity_key=3U3D3H52.

12. "Reproductive Justice," Sister Song, https://www.sistersong.net/reproductive-justice.

13. Errin Haines, "The Fights for the Vote and Bodily Autonomy Are Connected. So Are the Women Who Are Telling Us How," *19th*, October 28, 2022, https://19thnews .org/2022/10/women-of-color-democracy-voting-abortion-efforts/.

14. Leah Litman, Melissa Murray, and Kate Shaw, "The Link Between Voting Rights and the Abortion Ruling," *Washington Post*, June 28, 2022.

15. Ayanna Pressley, "When I say . . ." (tweet), Twitter, June 30, 2018, https:// twitter.com/AyannaPressley/status/1013184081696346113.

16. Rosalind Early, "The Sweat and Blood of Fannie Lou Hamer," *Humanities* 42, no. 1 (Winter 2021), https://www.neh.gov/article/sweat-and-blood-fannie -lou-hamer.

ON VOTING ACCESS

1. Chiraag Bains, "Honor the Voting Rights Act by Restoring Its Anti-Racist Core," Demos, August 6, 2019, https://www.demos.org/blog/honor-voting -rights-act-restoring-its-anti-racist-core.

2. Ari Berman, *Give Us the Ballot: The Modern Struggle for Voting Rights in America* (New York: Picador/Farrar, Straus & Giroux, 2016).

3. "Introducing the Inclusive Democracy Agenda," Demos, n.d., https://www .demos.org/policy-briefs/introducing-inclusive-democracy-agenda.

4. Laura Williamson and Brenda Wright, "Right to Vote: The Case for Expanding the Right to Vote in the U.S. Constitution," Demos, August 26, 2020, https://www.demos.org/policy-briefs/right-vote-case-expanding-right-vote-us -constitution.

5. "Executive Order on Promoting Access to Voting," White House, March 7, 2021, https://www.whitehouse.gov/briefing-room/presidential -actions/2021/03/07/executive-order-on-promoting-access-to-voting/.

6. "How and Why the Federal Agencies Can Register Voters," Demos/ACLU, https://www.demos.org/campaign/how-and-why-federal-agencies-can -register-voters#Impact.

7. "Strengthening Democracy: A Progress Report on Federal Agency Action to Promote Access to Voting," March 2, 2023, https://www.demos.org/policy -briefs/strengthening-democracy-progress-report-federal-agency-action -promote-access-voting.

8. "Introducing the Inclusive Democracy Agenda," Demos, https://www .demos.org/policy-briefs/introducing-inclusive-democracy-agenda#Self -Determination.

9. Laura Williamson, "Self-Determination of Political Status for Washington DC and the Territories," Demos, February 9, 2021, https://www.demos.org/policy -briefs/self-determination-political-status-washington-dc-and-territories.

10. Laura Williamson, Alex Baptiste, and Stephany Rose Spaulding, "End the Filibuster: How a Relic of Jim Crow Could Block Our Progressive Agenda," Demos, March 9, 2021, https://www.demos.org/policy-briefs/end-filibuster -how-relic-jim-crow-could-block-our-progressive-agenda.

11. Sydney Kashiwagi, "Minnesota Governor Poised to Sign Bill That Would Speed Right to Vote for Ex-Felons," CNN, February 23, 2023.

12. Ida B. Wells-Barnett, "How Enfranchisement Stops Lynching," Guide to the Ida B. Wells Papers, 1884–1976, University of Chicago, https://pi.lib .uchicago.edu/1001/scrc/ead/ICU.SPCL.IBWELLS.

13. "An Economy for All: Building a 'Black Women Best' Legislative Agenda," Congressional Caucus on Black Women and Girls, https://watsoncoleman .house.gov/imo/media/doc/bwb_report_2022_new.pdf.

14. Taifa Smith Butler, "Georgia Won't Thrive If People Don't Survive," Georgia Budget and Policy Institute, November 17, 2020, https://gbpi.org/georgia -wont-thrive-if-people-dont-survive/.

15. "Building Civic Power and Practicing Co-Governance: Equitable Access to

Flood Recovery in Harris County, TX," Demos, March 29, 2022, https://www.demos.org/research/building-civic-power-practicing-co-governance-equitable-access-flood-recovery-harris.

16. "Unstacking the Deck," Demos, June 22, 2021, https://www.demos.org/research/unstacking-deck.

17. Rick Hasen, "New Filings Reveal Another Billionaire Behind the Big Lie," Election Law Blog, January 20, 2022, https://electionlawblog.org/?p=127060; "Peter Thiel's Midterm Bet: The Billionaire Seeking to Disrupt America's Democracy," *Guardian*, October 15, 2022.

ON REPARATIONS

1. Ali Vitali, Kasie Hunt, and Frank Thorp V, "Trump Referred to Haiti and African Nations as 'Shithole' Countries," NBC News, January 12, 2018; Sherrilyn Ifill, "When Trump Attacks One Black Woman, We All Feel It," *Washington Post*, November 13, 2018; April Ryan, "I'm a Black Woman. Trump Loves Insulting People Like Me," *Washington Post*, November 10, 2018.

2. Adam Edelman, "Mother-Daughter Election Workers Targeted by Trump Say There's 'Nowhere' They Feel Safe," NBC News, June 21, 2022.

3. W. E. B. Du Bois, *Black Reconstruction in America* (New York: Simon & Schuster, 1995), 626.

4. Commission to Study and Develop Reparation Proposals for African Americans Act, H.R. 40, 117th Cong. (2021), https://www.congress.gov/bill/117th-congress/house-bill/40/text.

5. "After More Than a Century of Trying, Congress Passes an Anti-Lynching Bill," NPR, March 7, 2022.

6. Keisha N. Blain, *Until I Am Free: Fannie Lou Hamer's Enduring Message to America* (Boston: Beacon Press, 2021).

7. Kristin McIntosh et al., "Examining the Black-White Wealth Gap," Brookings Institution, February 27, 2020, https://www.brookings.edu/blog/up-front/2020/02/27/examining-the-black-white-wealth-gap/.

ON DISABILITY AND THE AMERICAN DREAM

1. For an overview of the ADA, see William D. Goren, *Understanding the Americans with Disabilities Act* (Chicago: American Bar Association, 2013).

2. Hani Morgan, "Misunderstood and Mistreated: Students of Color in Special Education," *Voices of Reform* 3, no. 2 (December 2020): 71–81.

ON REPRODUCTIVE RIGHTS

1. Jael Silliman et al., *Undivided Rights: Women of Color Organize for Reproductive Justice*, 2nd ed. (Chicago: Haymarket Books, 2016), 55, 111, 166, 225–29.

2. Emily DiMatteo et al., "Reproductive Justice for Disabled Women: Ending Systemic Discrimination," Center for American Progress, April 13, 2022,

https://www.americanprogress.org/article/reproductive-justice-for-disabled-women-ending-systemic-discrimination/. On "breeders" and the South Carolina judge, see Angela Davis, *Women, Race, and Class* (New York: Vintage Books, 1983), 7. On Andrew Jackson, see David Stannard, *American Holocaust* (Oxford: Oxford University Press, 1992), 121. On Asian immigration policies, see Sucheta Mazumdar, "General Introduction: A Woman-Centered Perspective on Asian American History," in *Making Waves: An Anthology of Writings by and About Asian American Women*, ed. Asian Women United of California (Boston: Beacon Press, 1989), 2.

3. Anna Bernstein and Kelly M. Jones, *The Economic Effects of Contraceptive Access: A Review of the Evidence* (Washington, D.C.: Institute for Women's Policy Research, 2019), https://iwpr.org/wp-content/uploads/2020/07/B381_Contraception-Access_Final.pdf.

4. Loretta Ross, *Reproductive Justice: An Introduction* (Oakland: University of California Press, 2017).

5. Alina Salganicoff, Laurie Sobel, and Amrutha Ramaswamy, "The Hyde Amendment and Coverage for Abortion Services," KFF, March 5, 2021, https://www.kff.org/womens-health-policy/issue-brief/the-hyde-amendment-and-coverage-for-abortion-services/.

6. Office of Minority Health and Health Equity, "Working Together to Reduce Black Maternal Mortality," Centers for Disease Control and Prevention, April 6, 2022, https://www.cdc.gov/healthequity/features/maternal-mortality/index.html.

7. Diana Greene Foster et al., "The Harms of Denying a Woman a Wanted Abortion: Findings from the Turnaway Study," Advancing New Standards in Reproductive Health, April 16, 2020, University of California, San Francisco, https://www.ansirh.org/sites/default/files/publications/files/the_harms_of_denying_a_woman_a_wanted_abortion_4-16-2020.pdf.

ON RACE AND DISABILITY

1. Janell Hobson, "Of 'Sound' and 'Unsound' Body and Mind: Reconfiguring the Heroic Portrait of Harriet Tubman," *Frontiers: A Journal of Women Studies* 40, no. 2 (2019): 193–218; Keisha N. Blain, *Until I Am Free: Fannie Lou Hamer's Enduring Message to America* (Boston: Beacon Press, 2021); and Eliza Suggs, *Shadow and Sunshine*, 21st ed. (1906; reprinted Chapel Hill: University of North Carolina Press, 1998), Documenting the American South, https://docsouth.unc.edu/neh/suggs/suggs.html.

2. Jenifer L. Barclay, "Mothering the 'Useless': Black Motherhood, Disability, and Slavery," *Women, Gender, and Families of Color* 2, no. 2 (Fall 2014): 117–18, 128–29.

3. Barclay, "Mothering the 'Useless'," 129; Millie McKoy and Christine McKoy, *The History of the Carolina Twins: Told in "Their Own Peculiar Way" by "One of Them"* (Buffalo, N.Y.: Buffalo Courier Printing House, n.d.), Documenting the American South, https://docsouth.unc.edu/neh/millie-christine/millie-christine.html.

4. Vilissa Thompson, "Removing Economic Barriers for Disabled People Requires Understanding Intersectionality," Century Foundation, May 25, 2022, https://tcf.org/content/commentary/removing-economic-barriers-for -disabled-people-requires-understanding-intersectionality/; Rebecca Vallas et al., *Economic Justice Is Disability Justice* (New York: Century Foundation, 2022), https://tcf.org/content/report/economic-justice-disability-justice/.

5. Vallas et al., *Economic Justice.*

6. David M. Perry and Lawrence Carter-Long, *On Media Coverage of Law Enforcement Use of Force and Disability*, Ruderman White Paper (Boston: Ruderman Family Foundation, 2016), https://rudermanfoundation.org/wp -content/uploads/2017/08/MediaStudy-PoliceDisability_final-final.pdf.

7. Sarah Blahovec, "Confronting the Whitewashing of Disability: Interview with #DisabilityTooWhite Creator Vilissa Thompson," *HuffPost*, June 28, 2016.

8. Vilissa Thompson, "Black Disabled Mothers Deserve to Be Seen, Especially on Mother's Day," *Prism*, May 7, 2021, https://prismreports.org/2021/05/07/ black-disabled-mothers-deserve-to-be-seen-especially-on-mothers-day/.

9. Lily Roberts, Mia Ives-Rublee, and Rose Khattar, "COVID-19 Likely Resulted in 1.2 Million More Disabled People by the End of 2021—Workplaces and Policy Will Need to Adapt," Center for American Progress, February 9, 2022, https://www.americanprogress.org/article/covid-19-likely-resulted-in-1-2 -million-more-disabled-people-by-the-end-of-2021-workplaces-and-policy -will-need-to-adapt/.

ON TRANSGENDER RIGHTS

1. *Covering LGBTQ Athletes at the 2020 Olympics and Paralympics* (Los Angeles: GLAAD, 2021), https://www.glaad.org/sites/default/files/GLAADOlympics MediaGuide.pdf.

2. Moises Mendez II, "Laverne Cox on What's Changed Since the 'Transgender Tipping Point,'" *Time*, February 28, 2023.

3. "Record Number of LGBT Characters on U.S. TV, Study Says," BBC, February 18, 2022.

4. Raquel Willis, "Welcome to the Age of Trans Political Power," *them*, November 13, 2017, https://www.them.us/story/welcome-to-the-age-of-trans-political-power.

5. Sydney Bauer, "Transgender Representation to Nearly Double in State Legislatures," NBC News, November 6, 2020.

6. Jeffrey M. Jones, "LGBT Identification in U.S. Ticks Up to 7.1%," *Gallup News*, February 17, 2022, https://news.gallup.com/poll/389792/lgbt -identification-ticks-up.aspx.

7. Nico Lang, "2022 Was the Worst Year Ever for Anti-Trans Bills, How Did We Get Here?," *them*, December 29, 2022, https://www.them.us/story/2022-anti -trans-bills-history-explained.

8. Hannah Becker et al., "Deaths in the Family," *Insider*, November 17, 2022, https://www.insider.com/transgender-violence-deaths-database-murder-cases -2017-2021.

9. Steve Endean, *Bringing Lesbian and Gay Rights into the Mainstream: Twenty Years of Progress*, ed. Vicki L. Eaklor (New York: Harrington Park Press, 2006), 120–21, 236, 276–77.

10. Endean, *Bringing Lesbian and Gay Rights into the Mainstream*, 31–33.

11. Janice G. Raymond, *The Transsexual Empire: The Making of the She-Male* (Boston: Beacon Press, 1979).

12. Bayard Rustin to Joseph Beam, April 21, 1986 in *I Must Resist: Bayard Rustin's Life in Letters*, ed. Michael G. Long (San Francisco: City Lights Books, 2012), 460–61.

13. "Fact Sheet: Employment Non-Discrimination Act," ACLU, n.d., https://www.aclu.org/other/fact-sheet-employment-non-discrimination-act.

14. Thee Santos, Caroline Medina, and Sharita Gruberg, "What You Need to Know About the Equality Act," Center for American Progress, March 15, 2021, https://www.americanprogress.org/article/need-know-equality-act/.

ON POLITICAL REPRESENTATION

1. Alistair Cooke, *Alistair Cooke's America* (New York: Knopf, 1973).

2. On the lynching, see James H. Madison, *A Lynching in the Heartland: Race and Memory in America* (New York: Palgrave Macmillan, 2001).

3. Phillis Wheatley to Samson Occom, February 11, 1774, in Wheatley, *Complete Writings*, ed. Vincent Carretta (New York: Penguin Books, 2001).

4. Darlene Superville, "Biden Signs Bill Making Lynching a Federal Hate Crime," Associated Press, March 29, 2022.

5. On Wells-Barnett, see Mia Bay, *To Tell the Truth Freely: The Life of Ida B. Wells* (New York: Hill & Wang, 2009); Paula Giddings, *Ida: A Sword Among Lions: Ida B. Wells and the Campaign Against Lynching* (New York: HarperCollins, 2008); Patricia Schechter, *Ida B. Wells-Barnett and American Reform 1880–1930* (Chapel Hill: University of North Carolina Press, 2001).

6. McKenzie Jean-Philippe, "9 Essential Angela Davis Books to Add to Your Shelf," *Oprah Daily*, June 8, 2020, https://www.oprahdaily.com/entertainment/books/g32803115/angela-davis-books/.

7. "Introducing the Inclusive Democracy Agenda," Demos, n.d., https://www.demos.org/policy-briefs/introducing-inclusive-democracy-agenda.

8. United Nations General Assembly Resolution 2200A, "International Covenant on Civil and Political Rights," Office of the High Commissioner for Human Rights, December 16, 1966, https://www.ohchr.org/en/instruments-mechanisms/instruments/international-covenant-civil-and-political-rights.

9. bell hooks, *Killing Rage: Ending Racism* (New York: Henry Holt, 1996), 262.

ON RACIAL INEQUITIES IN HEALTH CARE

1. Shameek Rakshit et al., "How Does U.S. Life Expectancy Compare to Other Countries?," Peterson-KFF Health System Tracker, December 6, 2022,

https://www.healthsystemtracker.org/chart-collection/u-s-life-expectancy
-compare-countries/.

2. "Life Expectancy at Birth, Total (Years)," World Bank, n.d., https://data
.worldbank.org/indicator/SP.DYN.LE00.IN?most_recent_value_desc=true.

3. CDC National Center for Health Statistics, "Life Expectancy Dropped for
the Second Year in a Row in 2021," Centers for Disease Control and Prevention, August 31, 2022, https://www.cdc.gov/nchs/pressroom/nchs_press_
releases/2022/20220831.htm.

4. "Timothy Snyder Speaks, ep. 4: Sadopopulism" (video), YouTube, December
2, 2017, https://www.youtube.com/watch?v=oOjJtEkKMX4.

5. Margaret Whitehead, "The Concepts and Principles of Equity in Health,"
International Journal of Health Services 22, no. 3 (1992): 429–45.

6. Aria Bendix, "Polio Detected in New York City Wastewater," NBC News,
August 12, 2022; Jacqueline Howard, "Measles Outbreak in Central Ohio
Grows to More Than 50 Children, Driven by 'Lack of Vaccination,'" CNN,
December 7, 2022.

7. Elizabeth Arias et al., *Provisional Life Expectancy Estimates for 2021* (Thousand Oaks, Calif.: National Vital Statistics System, 2022), https://www
.cdc.gov/nchs/data/vsrr/vsrr023.pdf; Rakshit et al., "How Does U.S. Life
Expectancy Compare"; "Life Expectancy," Peterson-KFF Health System
Tracker, https://www.healthsystemtracker.org/indicator/health-well-being/
life-expectancy/; CDC National Center for Health Statistics, "Life Expectancy Dropped."

8. Thomas C. Holt, *The Problem of Race in the Twenty-First Century* (Cambridge,
Mass.: Harvard University Press, 2000), 108.

9. Chiquita Brook-LaSure and Daniel Tsai, "A Strategic Vision for Medicaid and
the Children's Health Insurance Program (CHIP)," *Health Affairs Forefront*,
November 16, 2021, https://www.healthaffairs.org/do/10.1377/forefront
.20211115.537685/; Medicaid and CHIP Enrollment Data, "November
2022 Medicaid & CHIP Enrollment Data Highlights," Medicaid.gov, n.d.,
https://www.medicaid.gov/medicaid/program-information/medicaid-and
-chip-enrollment-data/report-highlights/index.html.

10. Brian P. Lee, Jennifer L. Dodge, and Norah A. Terrault, "Medicaid Expansion
and Variability in Mortality in the USA: A National, Observational Cohort
Study," *Lancet Public Health* 7, no. 1 (January 2022), https://www.thelancet
.com/journals/lanpub/article/PIIS2468-2667(21)00252-8/fulltext.

11. Sarah Miller, Norman Johnson, and Laura R. Wherry, "Medicaid and Mortality: New Evidence From Linked Survey and Administrative Data," *Quarterly
Journal of Economics* 136, no. 3 (August 2021): 1783–829; Steffie Woolhan-
dler and David U. Himmelstein, "The Relationship of Health Insurance and
Mortality: Is Lack of Insurance Deadly?," *Annals of Internal Medicine* 167,
no. 6 (September 2017): 424–31, https://www.acpjournals.org/doi/epdf/10
.7326/M17-1403; David W. Brown, Amanda E. Kowalski, and Ithai Z. Lurie,
"Medicaid as an Investment in Children: What Is the Long-Term Impact on

Tax Receipts?," National Bureau of Economic Research, Working Paper no. 20835, January 2015, https://www.nber.org/papers/w20835.

12. National Health Expenditure Data, "Historical," Centers for Medicare and Medicaid Services, n.d., https://www.cms.gov/research-statistics-data-and -systems/statistics-trends-and-reports/nationalhealthexpenddata/nationalheal thaccountshistorical.

13. "Public's Top Priority for 2022: Strengthening the Nation's Economy," Pew Research Center, February 16, 2022, https://www.pewresearch.org/ politics/2022/02/16/publics-top-priority-for-2022-strengthening-the -nations-economy/.

ON COALITION BUILDING

1. Josh Kraushaar, "Big Barrier to Black Representation in Congress Rapidly Declines," *Axios*, February 5, 2023, https://www.axios.com/2023/02/05/ black-lawmakers-118th-congress-influence.

2. "Declaration of Independence: A Transcription," National Archives, https:// www.archives.gov/founding-docs/declaration-transcript.

3. Lina Mann, "The Enslaved Household of President Thomas Jefferson," White House Historical Association, November 20, 2019, https://www .whitehousehistory.org/slavery-in-the-thomas-jefferson-white-house.

4. Mark Maloy, "The Founding Fathers, Views of Slavery," American Battlefield Trust, February 1, 2022, https://www.battlefields.org/learn/articles/founding -fathers-views-slavery; Evan Andrews, "How Many U.S. Presidents Owned Enslaved People?," History Channel, September 3, 2019, https://www.history .com/news/how-many-u-s-presidents-owned-slaves.

5. Laila Kazmi and Stephen Hegg, "What Former Presidential Candidate Shirley Chisholm Said About Facing Gender Discrimination," *PBS NewsHour*, September 13, 2016.

6. "African American Senators," U.S. Senate, https://www.senate.gov/ pagelayout/history/h_multi_sections_and_teasers/Photo_Exhibit_African_ American_Senators.htm.

7. Kelly Dittmar, "Women in Election 2022: Making Midterm Progress," Center for American Women and Politics, Eagleton Institute of Politics at Rutgers University, 2022, https://womenrun.rutgers.edu/2022-report/statewide -elective-executive-office/.

8. "Black Women in Elective Office," Center for American Women and Politics, Eagleton Institute of Politics at Rutgers University, n.d., https://cawp.rutgers .edu/black-women-elective-office.

9. Carrie Johnson, "President Biden Has Made Choosing Diverse Federal Judges a Priority," NPR, January 2, 2023.

10. "Fact Sheet: The John Lewis Voting Rights Advancement Act," Brennan Center for Justice, n.d., https://www.brennancenter.org/sites/default/files/2021 -12/VRAA_FactSheet.pdf.

11. Henry J. Gomez, "Here's What the George Floyd Justice in Policing Act Would Do," NBC News, April 21, 2021.

ON EQUAL PAY FOR BLACK WOMEN

1. Minda Harts, "Black Women's Equal Pay Day: Black Women Work 579 Days to Earn What White Men Do in 365," MSNBC, August 2, 2021.
2. See Chad Williams, *Torchbearers of Democracy: African American Soldiers in the World War I Era* (Chapel Hill: University of North Carolina Press, 2010).
3. See David R. Roediger, *The Wages of Whiteness: Race and the Making of the American Working Class*, rev. ed. (New York: Verso, 1999).
4. Ira Katznelson, *When Affirmative Action Was White: An Untold History of Racial Inequality in Twentieth-Century America* (New York: W.W. Norton, 2005).
5. Keisha N. Blain, "Black Political Rights Can't Be Divorced From Economic Justice. Why Fannie Lou Hamer's Message and Fight Endure Today," *Time*, October 27, 2021.
6. Shirley Chisholm, "For the Equal Rights Amendment," American Rhetoric, August 7, 2021, https://www.americanrhetoric.com/speeches/shirley chisholmequalrights.htm.
7. Robin Bleiweis, Jocelyn Frye, and Rose Khattar, "Women of Color and the Wage Gap," Center for American Progress, November 17, 2021, https://www .americanprogress.org/article/women-of-color-and-the-wage-gap/.
8. Congressional Caucus on Black Women and Girls, "Congressional Caucus on Black Women and Girls Co-Chairs Issue Statement on Black Women's Equal Pay Day," Office of Congresswoman Yvette D. Clarke, August 3, 2021, https://clarke.house.gov/congressional-caucus-on-black-women-and-girls-co -chairs-issue-statement-on-black-womens-equal-pay-day/.
9. Morgan Smith, "How the Pandemic Made the Pay Gap Worse for Low-Wage Workers and Women of Color," CNBC, March 15, 2022.
10. Jasmine Tucker, "Men Have Now Recouped Their Pandemic-Related Labor Force Losses While Women Lag Behind," National Women's Law Center, February 2022 Fact Sheet, https://nwlc.org/wp-content/uploads/2022/02/ January-Jobs-Day-updated.pdf.
11. Claire Ewing-Nelson and Jasmine Tucker, "Only About One Third of the 916,000 Jobs Gained Last Month Went to Women," National Women's Law Center, April 2021 Fact Sheet, https://nwlc.org/wp-content/ uploads/2021/04/March-Jobs-Day-2021-v1-1.pdf.
12. "About Us," Higher Heights for America PAC, n.d., https://www .higherheightsforamericapac.org/about-us/.
13. Jasmine Mithani, "The United States Just Hit Equal Pay Day for Black Women," *19th*, September 21, 2022, https://19thnews.org/2022/09/black -women-equal-pay-day/.
14. "Black Women and the Wage Gap," National Partnership for Women and Families, October 2022 Fact Sheet, https://www.nationalpartnership.org/our-work/ resources/economic-justice/fair-pay/african-american-women-wage-gap.pdf.

15. "The Paycheck Fairness Act," National Partnership for Women and Families, March 2023 Fact Sheet, https://www.nationalpartnership.org/our-work/resources/economic-justice/fair-pay/the-paycheck-fairness-act.pdf.

16. "The House Passes the Paycheck Fairness Act, in a Victory for Equal Pay," National Women's Law Center, April 15, 2021, https://nwlc.org/press-release/the-house-passes-the-paycheck-fairness-act-in-a-victory-for-equal-pay/.

17. "Adams, Warnock Introduce Black Women's Equal Pay Day Resolution," Office of Congresswoman Alma Adams, August 3, 2021, https://adams.house.gov/media-center/press-releases/adams-warnock-introduce-black-womens-equal-pay-day-resolution.

18. Kamala Harris, "Remarks by Vice President Harris at the Equal Pay Day Summit," White House Briefing Room, March 15, 2022, https://www.whitehouse.gov/briefing-room/speeches-remarks/2022/03/15/remarks-by-vice-president-harris-at-the-equal-pay-day-summit/.

ON POLITICAL POWER

1. Martin Luther King, Jr., "Where Do We Go From Here?" (speech), August 16, 1967, Martin Luther King, Jr. Research and Education Institute, Stanford University, https://kinginstitute.stanford.edu/where-do-we-go-here.

2. Antonio Gramsci, *Prison Notebooks*, trans and ed. Joseph A. Buttigieg, trans. Antonio Callari (New York: Columbia University Press, 2011).

3. Ai-jen Poo, interview, *Unladylike2020: The Changemakers*, American Masters Digital Archive (WNET), October 17, 2019, PBS, https://www.pbs.org/wnet/americanmasters/archive/interview/ai-jen-poo/; Miriam Axel-Lute, "Interview with Ai-jen Poo, Director of the National Domestic Workers Alliance," *Shelterforce*, May 30, 2015, https://shelterforce.org/2015/05/30/interview_with_ai-jen_poo/.

4. King, "Where Do We Go From Here?"

5. Alicia Lee, "Congressional Democrats Criticized for Wearing Kente Cloth at Event Honoring George Floyd," CNN, June 8, 2020.

6. Rashad Robinson, interview by Ashley C. Ford, *Into the Mix* (podcast transcript), May 25, 2022, Vox Creative, https://www.vox.com/ad/23138342/into-the-mix-episode-6.

7. Mark Knoller, "A Look Back to 2005: President Bush and Katrina," *CBS News*, August 29, 2010.

ON BLACK WOMEN'S ELECTORAL POWER

1. Holly Otterbein and Elena Schneider, "Democrats Growing Anxious—Again—Over Black Turnout," Politico, October 12, 2022.

2. "2017 Elections Alabama Senate," CNN, n.d., https://www.cnn.com/election/2017/results/alabama-senate.

3. Ina Jaffe, "For Older Voters, Getting the Right ID Can Be Especially Tough," NPR, September 7, 2018.

4. Lynette Hazelton, "Getting Souls Out to the Polls," *Philadelphia Inquirer*, November 7, 2022.

5. "About the AECST," African Episcopal Church of St. Thomas, n.d., http://www.aecst.org/about.htm.

6. Nannie H. Burroughs, "How the Sisters Are Hindered from Helping," September 13, 1900, Archive of Women's Political Communication, Iowa State University, https://awpc.cattcenter.iastate.edu/2019/09/26/how-the-sisters-are-hindered-from-helping/.

7. Allison Calhoun-Brown, "Upon This Rock: The Black Church, Nonviolence, and the Civil Rights Movement," *PS: Political Science & Politics* 33, no. 2 (2000): 169–74.

8. Besheer Mohamed et al., "Faith Among Black Americans," Pew Research Center, March 1, 2023, https://www.pewresearch.org/religion/2021/02/16/faith-among-black-americans/.

9. Nannie H. Burroughs, "Black Women and Reform," August 1, 1915, Archive of Women's Political Communication. Iowa State University, https://awpc.cattcenter.iastate.edu/2019/09/27/black-women-and-reform/.

ON EQUITY IN EDUCATION

1. Linda Darling-Hammond, "Unequal Opportunity: Race and Education," Brookings Institution, March 1, 1998, https://www.brookings.edu/articles/unequal-opportunity-race-and-education/; Emma Garcia, "Schools Are Still Segregated and Black Children Are Paying the Price," Economy Policy Institute, February 12, 2020, https://www.epi.org/publication/schools-are-still-segregated-and-black-children-are-paying-a-price/.

2. Jarvis Givens, *Fugitive Pedagogy: Carter G. Woodson and the Art of Black Teaching* (Cambridge, Mass.: Harvard University Press, 2021).

3. Zebulon Vance Miletsky, *Before Busing: A History of Boston's Long Black Freedom Struggle* (Chapel Hill: University of North Carolina Press, 2021).

ON FREEDOM FROM POLICING

1. White House Briefing Room, "Fact Sheet: President Biden's Safer America Plan" (press release), August 1, 2022, https://www.whitehouse.gov/briefing-room/statements-releases/2022/08/01/fact-sheet-president-bidens-safer-america-plan-2/.

2. Katherine Leach-Kemon and Rebecca Sirull, "On Gun Violence, the United States Is an Outlier," IHME, May 31, 2022, https://www.healthdata.org/acting-data/gun-violence-united-states-outlier.

3. Jennifer Tolbert, Patrick Drake, and Anthony Damico, "Key Facts about the Uninsured Population," KFF, December 19, 2022, https://www.kff.org/uninsured/issue-brief/key-facts-about-the-uninsured-population/.

4. Munira Z. Gunja, Evan D. Gumas, and Reginald D. Williams II, "The U.S. Maternal Mortality Crisis Continues to Worsen: An International

Comparison," Commonwealth Fund, December 1, 2022, https://www.commonwealthfund.org/blog/2022/us-maternal-mortality-crisis-continues-worsen-international-comparison.

5. U.S. Department of Housing and Urban Development, "HUD Releases 2022 Annual Homeless Assessment Report" (press release), HUD No. 22–253, December 19, 2022, https://www.hud.gov/press/press_releases_media_advisories/HUD_No_22_253.

6. Robert H. Shmerling, "Why Life Expectancy in the U.S. Is Falling," Harvard Health Publishing, October 20, 2022, https://www.health.harvard.edu/blog/why-life-expectancy-in-the-us-is-falling-202210202835.

7. Jake Horton, "Does U.S. Really Have World's Highest Covid Death Toll?," *BBC News*, May 12, 2022; Benjamin Mueller and Eleanor Lutz, "U.S. Has Far Higher Covid Death Rate Than Other Wealthy Countries," *New York Times*, February 1, 2022.

8. "United States Profile," Prison Policy Initiative, n.d., https://www.prisonpolicy.org/profiles/US.html.

9. Anagha Srikanth, "Black People 5 Times More Likely to Be Arrested Than Whites, According to New Analysis," *Hill*, June 11, 2020, https://thehill.com/changing-america/respect/equality/502277-black-people-5-times-more-likely-to-be-arrested-than-whites/.

10. Robert Brame et al., "Demographic Patterns of Cumulative Arrest Prevalence by Ages 18 and 23," *Crime and Delinquency* 60, no. 3 (2014): 471–86, https://www.ncbi.nlm.nih.gov/pmc/articles/PMC4443707/.

11. James Baldwin, "James Baldwin Discusses His Book *Nobody Knows My Name: More Notes of a Native Son*," interview by Studs Terkel (transcript), WFMT, Studs Terkel Radio Archive, July 15, 1961, https://studsterkel.wfmt.com/programs/james-baldwin-discusses-his-book-nobody-knows-my-name-more-notes-native-son.

12. Rebecca Solnit, *A Paradise Built in Hell: The Extraordinary Communities That Arise in Disaster* (New York: Penguin, 2010).

13. Dorothy Day, *From Union Square to Rome* (Silver Spring, Md.: Preservation of the Faith Press, 1938).

14. "What Policing Costs: A Look at Spending in America's Biggest Cities," Vera Institute of Justice, n.d., https://www.vera.org/publications/what-policing-costs-in-americas-biggest-cities.

15. Brenden Beck, "We Analyzed 29 Years of Police Spending in Hundreds of Cities," *Slate*, April 14, 2022.

16. Heather L. Sipsma et al., "Spending On Social and Public Health Services and Its Association with Homicide in the USA: An Ecological Study," *BMJ Open* 7, no. 10 (2017), https://bmjopen.bmj.com/content/7/10/e016379.

17. Daniel Rivkin, "Public School Investment Reduces Adult Crime, Study Shows," *University Record*, May 10, 2022, https://record.umich.edu/articles/public-school-investment-reduces-adult-crime-study-shows/; Mansai Deshpande and Michael Mueller-Smith, "Does Welfare Prevent Crime?: The Criminal Justice Outcomes of Youth Removed from SSI," *Quarterly Journal*

of Economics 137, no. 4 (November 2022): 2263–307, https://academic.oup .com/qje/article-abstract/137/4/2263/6581195.

18. Jahdziah St. Julien, "Community-Based Violence Interruption Programs Can Reduce Gun Violence," Center for American Progress, July 14, 2022, https:// www.americanprogress.org/article/community-based-violence-interruption -programs-can-reduce-gun-violence/.

19. "Solidarity Budget 2023: Budget to Live, Budget to Thrive," Seattle Solidarity Budget, https://www.seattlesolidaritybudget.com/solidarity-budget-2023.

20. "Solidarity Budget 2023."

21. "Solidarity Budget Wins Elimination of 80 'Ghost Cops' from City Budget, Protects Investments in Community Well-Being" (press release), Seattle Solidarity Budget, November 30, 2022, https://docs.google.com/document/ d/1fQ6EgLVC1h3bApvnpr-M1ISxvx_UJR5QYa70f8kH1y0/edit.

22. "Solidarity Budget 2023."

23. Ruth Wilson Gilmore, *Golden Gulag: Prisons, Surplus, Crisis, and Opposition in Globalizing California* (Oakland: University of California Press, 2007).

24. Mark Joseph Stern, "The Police Lie. All the Time. Can Anything Stop Them?," *Slate*, August 4, 2020.

25. Akerah Mackey with Marvin Slaughter, "No Amount of Training Can Prevent Police Brutality," *Chicago Policy Review*, April 19, 2021, https:// chicagopolicyreview.org/2021/04/19/no-amount-of-training-can-prevent -police-brutality/.

26. Damon Williams, interview by Kia Smith, "Who Are the Organizers?," *South Side Weekly*, September 16, 2020, https://southsideweekly.com/who-are-the -organizers/.

ON ECONOMIC JUSTICE

1. A. Philip Randolph Institute, *A "Freedom Budget" for All Americans: Budgeting Our Resources 1966–1975 to Achieve "Freedom from Want"* (New York: A. Philip Randolph Institute, 1966), 2–3.

2. For a broad overview of the Freedom Budget, see Paul Le Blanc and Michael D. Yates, *A Freedom Budget for All Americans: Recapturing the Promise of the Civil Rights Movement in the Struggle for Economic Justice Today* (New York: Monthly Review Press, 2013).

3. A. Philip Randolph, "Introduction" to Randolph Institute, *"Freedom Budget" for All.*

4. Randolph Institute, *"Freedom Budget" for All.*

5. Franklin D. Roosevelt, State of the Union Message to Congress, January 11, 1944, Franklin D. Roosevelt Presidential Library and Museum, https://www .fdrlibrary.org/address-text.

6. Cass R. Sunstein, *The Second Bill of Rights: FDR's Unfinished Revolution and Why We Need It More Than Ever* (New York: Basic Books, 2006).

7. Jessica Dickler, "63% of Americans Are Living Paycheck to Paycheck— Including Nearly Half of Six-Figure Earners," CNBC, October 24, 2022.

8. Michael Sainato, "'I'm Selling My Blood': Millions in US Can't Make Ends Meet with Two Jobs," *Guardian*, November 5, 2022.

9. Sapna Mehta, "America's Lack of Paid Leave Is Devastating Women and Families," *Ms.*, January 31, 2023; Jennifer Tolbert, Patrick Drake, and Anthony Damico, "Key Facts about the Uninsured Population," KFF, December 19, 2022, https://www.kff.org/uninsured/issue-brief/key-facts-about-the-uninsured-population/.

10. Ben Popken, "Millions of Kids Were Thrust Back into Poverty After the Child Tax Credit Expired. What's Next?," *NBC News*, January 25, 2022.

11. Nannie Helen Burroughs, "What Must the Negro Do to Be Saved?," *Louisiana Weekly*, December 23, 1933, Speaking While Female Speech Bank, https://speakingwhilefemale.co/race-burroughs2/.

ON ANTI-BLACKNESS

1. Charlene A. Carruthers, *Unapologetic: A Black, Queer, and Feminist Mandate for Radical Movements* (Boston: Beacon Press, 2018).

2. Cedric J. Robinson, *Black Marxism: The Making of the Black Radical Tradition*, 3rd ed. (Chapel Hill: University of North Carolina Press, 2020); Sylvia Wynter, "Unsettling the Coloniality of Being/Power/Truth/Freedom: Towards the Human, After Man, Its Overrepresentation—An Argument," *CR: New Centennial Review* 3, no. 3 (Fall 2003): 257–337.

3. Ruth Wilson Gilmore, *Change Everything: Racial Capitalism and the Case for Abolition* (Chicago: Haymarket Books, 2021).

4. For an excellent overview of Black feminist activism in both national and global contexts, see Kimberly Springer, *Living for the Revolution: Black Feminist Organizations, 1968–1980* (Durham, N.C.: Duke University Press, 2005).

5. Springer, *Living for the Revolution,* 2.

6. Springer, *Living for the Revolution*, 2.

7. Springer, *Living for the Revolution*, 4.

8. Combahee River Collective, *The Combahee River Collective Statement: Black Feminist Organizing in the Seventies and Eighties* (Latham, N.Y.: Kitchen Table: Women of Color Press, 1986), 9.

9. Combahee River Collective, *Combahee River Collective Statement*, 15.

10. Combahee River Collective, *Combahee River Collective Statement*, 14.

11. Cary Barbor, "Florida Voting Rights Group Nominated for Nobel Peace Prize," WGCU, February 20, 2023, https://news.wgcu.org/section/social-justice/2023-02-20/florida-voting-rights-group-nominated-for-nobel-peace-prize; Ashley Lopez,. "Florida's Effort to Charge 20 People with Voter Fraud Has Hit Some Roadblocks," NPR, December 21, 2022.

12. See Madison Haussy, "Case Study: Participatory Budgeting in Brazil," *Updating Democracy//Rebooting the State*, *Medium*, April 5, 2021, https://medium.com/updating-democracy-rebooting-the-state/case-study-participatory-budgeting-in-brazil-9b7c48290c29; "PB's Impacts," Participatory Budgeting Project, n.d., https://www.participatorybudgeting.org/impacts/.

ON ANTI-LGBTQ+ VIOLENCE

1. Isabel Funk, "Local Transgender Activist Elise Malary's Death Ruled a Drowning," *Daily Northwestern*, June 16, 2022, https://dailynorthwestern .com/2022/06/16/city/local-transgender-activist-elise-malarys-death-ruled-a -drowning/.
2. Emma Specter, " 'I Believe in Black Trans Power': 15,000 Protestors Showed Up for a Consistently Marginalized Community," *Vogue*, June 15, 2020.
3. Imara Jones, "Why Black Trans Women Are Essential to Our Future," *Time*, August 20, 2020.
4. Brooke Migdon, "Black LGBTQ Representation Has More Than Quadrupled over Five Years, Report Finds," *Hill*, February 24, 2023, https://thehill .com/changing-america/respect/diversity-inclusion/3872710-black-lgbtq -representation-has-more-than-quadrupled-over-five-years-report-finds/.
5. Migdon, "Black LGBTQ Representation."

ON FAITH AND LOVE

1. On the history of the Black national anthem, see Imani Perry, *May We Forever Stand: A History of the Black National Anthem* (Chapel Hill: University of North Carolina Press, 2018).
2. Martin Luther King, Jr., *Strength to Love* (Philadelphia: Fortress Press, 1963), 70.
3. Sandeep Ravindran, "Researchers Find That Modern Humans Originated in Southern Africa," *Stanford Medicine*, March 13, 2011, https://med .stanford.edu/news/all-news/2011/03/researchers-find-that-modern-humans -originated-in-southern-africa.html.
4. Jacqui Lewis, *Fierce Love: A Bold Path to Ferocious Courage and Rule-Breaking Kindness That Can Heal the World* (New York: Harmony Books, 2021).
5. "In U.S., Decline of Christianity Continues at Rapid Pace," Pew Research Center, October 17, 2019, https://www.pewresearch.org/religion/2019/10/17/in -u-s-decline-of-christianity-continues-at-rapid-pace/.
6. Ta-Nehisi Coates, "The Case for Reparations," *Atlantic*, June 2014.

ON VIOLENCE AGAINST BLACK WOMEN

1. Treva B. Lindsey, *America, Goddam: Violence, Black Women, and the Struggle for Justice* (Oakland: University of California Press, 2022).
2. Susan M. Latta, "Rebecca Lee Crumpler and Rebecca Cole: The First African American Women Physicians," in *Bold Women in Medicine: 21 Stories of Astounding Discoveries, Daring Surgeries, and Healing Breakthroughs*, ed. Susan M. Latta (Chicago: Chicago Review Press, 2017).
3. On the societal disparities facing Black girls in the United States, see Monique Morris, *Pushout: The Criminalization of Black Girls in Schools* (New York: New Press, 2018).

ON RACISM AND FATPHOBIA

1. Lulu Heffernan, "Black Feminist Brittney Cooper Urges UP Community to 'Trust Black Women,'" *Beacon*, September 9, 2020, https://www.upbeacon.com/article/2020/09/trust-black-women.
2. "Obesity and African Americans," Office of Minority Health, March 26, 2020, https://minorityhealth.hhs.gov/omh/browse.aspx?lvl=4&lvlid=25.
3. Tami Sawyer, "Singing loud and proud! I think my voice is a mix between Ariel and Aaliyah but what it's saying is 'You racists losing your jobssssssss'" (post), Facebook, November 6, 2020, https://www.facebook.com/tamisawyer/posts/10103151603034140.
4. Sabrina Strings, *Fearing the Black Body: The Racial Origins of Fat Phobia* (New York: New York University Press, 2019), 6.
5. Strings, *Fearing the Black Body*, 90–99.
6. Strings, *Fearing the Black Body*, 140–46, 148–49, 153–57, 198–99.
7. Karma R. Chávez, "The Body: An Abstract and Actual Rhetorical Concept," *Rhetoric Society Quarterly* 48, no. 3 (2018): 242–50.
8. Chávez, "The Body," 247; Maegan Parker Brooks, *A Voice That Could Stir An Army: Fannie Lou Hamer and the Rhetoric of the Black Freedom Movement* (Jackson: University Press of Mississippi, 2014), 82, 87.
9. Brittney Cooper, "I'm reminded that in the 19th century Black women used sex strikes" (tweet), Twitter, October 15, 2020, https://twitter.com/ProfessorCrunk/status/1316798466962714624.
10. Tonyaa Weathersbee, "Weathersbee: Racist Caricatures Give Comfort to Bigots Looking to Marginalize Black Women," *Commercial Appeal* (Memphis), September 1, 2019, https://www.commercialappeal.com/story/news/2019/09/02/memphis-magazine-tami-sawyer-caricature-cover-tonyaa-weathersbeen/2187162001/.
11. Deborah Douglas, "Social Media Erupts over Depiction of Mayoral Candidate Tami Sawyer," MLK50, August 31, 2019, https://mlk50.com/2019/08/31/social-media-erupts-over-depiction-of-mayoral-candidate-tami-sawyer/.
12. Moya Bailey, *Misogynoir Transformed: Black Women's Digital Resistance* (New York: New York University Press, 2021).
13. Tressie McMillan Cottom, "Trust Black Women?," *Some of Us Are Brave*, n.d., https://tressiemc.com/uncategorized/trust-black-women/.

INDEX